שומרי מצוה

בני מצוה

by Joel Lurie Grishaver & Jane Golub

Artwork by Lane Yerkes, Christine Tripp
Mark Robert Halper

Siddur Mastery & Meaning
Volume 3

ISBN #1-891662-25-2

Copyright © 2003 Torah Aura Productions
Artwork © Christine Tripp
Artwork © Lane Yerkes
Icon Photographs © Mark Robert Halper

Torah Aura Productions • 4423 Fruitland Avenue, Los Angeles, CA 90058

(800) BE-Torah • (800) 238-6724 • (323) 585-7312 • fax (323) 585-0327

E-MAIL <misrad@torahaura.com> • Visit the Torah Aura website at www.torahaura.com

MANUFACTURED IN CANADA

Being at Mt. Sinai

God gave the Torah to Israel at Mt. Sinai. God gave it to Israel a second time as part of the teachings that were done in the Tabernacle. God then regave the Torah to them a third time when Israel was on the steppes of Moav. Israel actually received the Torah three times (*The Rokeakh, Ma'aseh Rokeakh*).

In the Talmud we are told that it is a mitzvah to read the סְדְרָה (the weekly Torah portion) three times in a week, twice in the original Hebrew and once in translation. We are then told that anyone who completes this third time with the congregation, as part of the communal reading, will be rewarded (*Brakhot* 8a/b).

When we study Torah with the congregation we are returning to Mt. Sinai (*The Rokeakh*).

In the Midrash we learn that every single Jew was at Mount Sinai and heard the Torah (*Midrash ha-Gadol*).

Rabbi Menahem Mendel of Kotzk taught: "Every Jew should try to imagine the event at Sinai" (*Emet v'Emunah*).

Rabbi Elimelekh of Lyzhansk said: "Not only do I remember being at Sinai, but I also remember who was standing next to me" (*Binat Ya'akov*).

Rabbi Kook taught: "When we pray we take that which is in us and reach up...When we study Torah we take the light from above and plant it in our deepest nature" (*Olat Re-iyah, Vol. 1, pp 19, 20*).

Questions

1. How is reading Torah in synagogue on Shabbat like being at Mount Sinai?
2. How do we "take the light from Torah and plant it in our deepest nature"?

> In this unit you will learn:
> • The idea of "being at Sinai."
> • The root יר ה

3

The Torah Service

Practice these phrases from the Torah service.

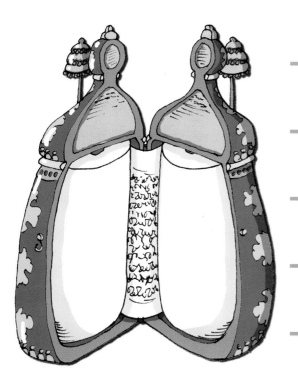

1. יי מֶלֶךְ יי מָלָךְ יי יִמְלֹךְ לְעוֹלָם וָעֶד

2. בָּרוּךְ שֶׁנָּתַן תּוֹרָה לְעַמּוֹ יִשְׂרָאֵל בִּקְדֻשָּׁתוֹ

3. כִּי מִצִּיּוֹן תֵּצֵא תוֹרָה וּדְבַר יי מִירוּשָׁלָיִם

4. אֶחָד אֱלֹהֵינוּ גָּדוֹל אֲדוֹנֵינוּ קָדוֹשׁ שְׁמוֹ

5. גַּדְּלוּ לַיי אִתִּי וּנְרוֹמְמָה שְׁמוֹ יַחְדָּו

6. אֵין כָּמוֹךָ בָאֱלֹהִים אֲדֹנָי וְאֵין כְּמַעֲשֶׂיךָ

7. וְזֹאת הַתּוֹרָה אֲשֶׁר שָׂם מֹשֶׁה לִפְנֵי בְּנֵי יִשְׂרָאֵל

8. עֵץ חַיִּים הִיא לַמַּחֲזִיקִים בָּהּ וְתוֹמְכֶיהָ מְאֻשָּׁר

9. הֲשִׁיבֵנוּ יי אֵלֶיךָ וְנָשׁוּבָה חַדֵּשׁ יָמֵינוּ כְּקֶדֶם

10. מַלְכוּתְךָ מַלְכוּת כָּל־עוֹלָמִים וּמֶמְשַׁלְתְּךָ בְּכָל־דּוֹר וָדוֹר

11. אַב הָרַחֲמִים הֵיטִיבָה בִרְצוֹנְךָ אֶת־צִיּוֹן תִּבְנֶה חוֹמוֹת יְרוּשָׁלָיִם

12. וַיְהִי בִּנְסֹעַ הָאָרֹן וַיֹּאמֶר מֹשֶׁה קוּמָה יי וְיָפֻצוּ אוֹיְבֶיךָ וְיָנֻסוּ מְשַׂנְאֶיךָ מִפָּנֶיךָ

The Torah Service Is Like...

The Torah service acts out the years that the Families-of-Israel spent wandering in the wilderness. In the Torah we are told Israel suffered because "they traveled three days in the wilderness and did not find water" (Exodus 15.22). The Talmud uses this verse to explain why we read Torah on Mondays, Thursdays, and Shabbat. It teaches that "Torah" is like "water," and we should never go more than three days without having a "drink of Torah."

(*Bava Kamma* 82a)

The Torah service is like being at Mt. Sinai when the Torah was given. Rabbi Joseph Soloveitchik taught that the Torah service is "a new giving of the Torah, the amazing standing under the mountain that burned with fire...each time we take out the Torah."

(*Halakhic Man*, pp. 227-8)

The Torah service is also a Torah class. In the Talmud, when Ezra makes it a rule that the Families-of-Israel will read Torah on Shabbat, he explains that this is because people who did not work in the marketplace on Mondays and Thursdays would miss their chance to learn Torah.

(*Bava Kamma* 82a)

Here are things we do during the Torah service. Put a **W** by all of those that recall the time in the wilderness. Put an **S** by all of those that recall being at Mt. Sinai. And put a **C** next to those things that connect the Torah reading to a class. Some of these things may have more than one letter next to them.

_____ We stand when the ark is opened.

_____ The Torah leads a procession around the synagogue.

_____ The congregation speaks words together.

_____ Everyone is ordered to listen during the Torah reading.

_____ A *D'var Torah* (lesson) is given.

_____ People touch the Torah with a prayerbook, hand, or טַלִּית and touch their lips.

5

Can you see the three letters ירה in these words?

מוֹרֶה תּוֹרָה יָרָה

Sometimes the י changes into a וֹ.

יָרָה = taught

תּוֹרָה = Torah

מוֹרֶה = teacher

Practice these words and phrases and circle all the words that contain the root ירה.

1. וְנָתַן לָנוּ אֶת־תּוֹרָתוֹ בָּרוּךְ אַתָּה יי נוֹתֵן הַתּוֹרָה

2. אֲשֶׁר נָתַן לָנוּ תּוֹרַת אֱמֶת וְחַיֵּי עוֹלָם נָטַע בְּתוֹכֵנוּ

3. כִּי מִצִּיּוֹן תֵּצֵא תוֹרָה וּדְבַר יי מִירוּשָׁלָיִם

4. כִּי לֶקַח טוֹב נָתַתִּי לָכֶם תּוֹרָתִי אַל תַּעֲזֹבוּ

5. בָּרוּךְ שֶׁנָּתַן תּוֹרָה לְעַמּוֹ יִשְׂרָאֵל בִּקְדֻשָּׁתוֹ

6. וְזֹאת הַתּוֹרָה אֲשֶׁר שָׂם מֹשֶׁה לִפְנֵי בְּנֵי יִשְׂרָאֵל עַל פִּי יי בְּיַד מֹשֶׁה

7. עַל הַתּוֹרָה וְעַל הָעֲבוֹדָה וְעַל הַנְּבִיאִים וְעַל יוֹם הַשַּׁבָּת הַזֶּה

"Just as the תּוֹרָה was given with awe and fear, so must we always treat it with awe and fear" (J. Talmud, Megillah 4.1).

6

The Torah Is Given Every Day

When God was teaching the Torah to Moses, God told him to put little crowns on the top of some letters. Making all those extra pen strokes was a lot of work. Moses asked God, "Why go to all this effort to put crowns on all these letters?"

God answered him, "In the future there is going to be a man, Akiva ben Yosef, who will learn things from the details of the crowns."

Moses demanded, "Take me to this man."

Moses was immediately zapped into Rabbi Akiva's school. He was placed in the last seat in the last row. This was the dunce seat. He listened to the lesson and could not understand a word that Rabbi Akiva was teaching. He felt like the dunce.

When the lesson ended, one of the students asked, "Rabbi, where did you learn this lesson?" Rabbi Akiva answered, "All this we learned from Moses *our teacher.*" Moses felt much better (*Avodah Zara* 19a).

How could Rabbi Akiva learn something in the Torah that Moses did not know? The Zohar teaches, "When a person speaks words of Torah, those words come before God. God takes those words and kisses them" (*Zohar* 1.4b).

Questions

1. Why do you think that Moses was confused by the lessons that Rabbi Akiva taught?
2. What do you think it means that God "kisses our words of Torah"?
3. How was Rabbi Akiva's school a part of Mt. Sinai? How is every day a day we can visit Mt. Sinai?

When I Was at Mt. Sinai...

The Families-of-Israel traveled from Raamses to Sukkot, about six hundred thousand of them on foot, and in addition, children. Also, a mixed multitude went out with them... and they baked matzah out of the dough that they had taken out of Egypt, it had not risen, since they had been driven out of Egypt and could not delay (Exodus 12.40-1).

1. When I left Egypt, one thing I took with me was:

_____

_____

_____

On the third month after the escape from Egypt the Families-of-Israel traveled from Refidim to the Wilderness of Sinai and camped there (Exodus 19.1).

2. One way my life changed when I left Egypt was:

עֲצֹר!

_____

_____

_____

When the Families-of-Israel camped at the foot of the Mountain, Moses went up to God. The Eternal said... "If you will listen carefully to My voice and if you will keep My Covenant...You will be a... holy people" (Exodus 19.2-6).

3. One reason I am worthy to receive the Torah is:

_____

_____

The Midrash teaches that *every Jew who ever lived was at Mt. Sinai* (Exodus Rabbah 28.5).

4. Three people who were standing near me were:

_____

_____

_____

Mt. Sinai was all in smoke because the Eternal came down in fire...the whole mountain shook a lot... The Eternal said all these things (Exodus 19.18-20).

5. When God taught you Torah, what did it sound like? _____

_____

8

Beginning the Torah Service

Unit 2

אֵין כָּמוֹךָ

The Torah service begins with the אֵין כָּמוֹךָ. These are words that are said before the ark is opened. It starts by praising God. It says:

- God is the Ultimate.
- God rules everywhere/everywhen.
- God was/is/always will be The Ruler.

אַב הָרַחֲמִים

The Torah service continues with אַב הָרַחֲמִים, which makes requests of God:

- Be good to Zion.
- Rebuild the walls of Jerusalem.

It ends by:

- Telling God, "We trust in You alone."
- Praising God as, "Ruler, high and exalted God, Master of Eternity."

In a moment we will rise and open the ark. The Torah will be taken out, and we will busy ourselves, first with the Torah as a symbol, and then with the Torah as words. Before there can be any confusion, before we can fool ourselves into thinking that it is the Torah we are worshiping, we start with God. We remember that Torah is a way of bringing God into our lives.

In this unit you will learn:

- 2 Prayers
- Roots: רצה, מלך   Word: אין
- Torah Service Images

9

Beginning the Torah Service

There is no God like YOU among the things that others think are gods,	אֵין כָּמוֹךָ בָאֱלֹהִים אֲדֹנָי	1.
There are no DOINGS like Yours.	וְאֵין כְּמַעֲשֶׂיךָ.	2.
Your EMPIRE is an EMPIRE for always,	מַלְכוּתְךָ מַלְכוּת כָּל־עוֹלָמִים	4.
Your RULE is for every generation.	וּמֶמְשַׁלְתְּךָ בְּכָל־דּוֹר וָדוֹר.	5.
ADONAI RULES. ADONAI has RULED. ADONAI will RULE	יי מֶלֶךְ יי מָלָךְ יי יִמְלֹךְ	6.
for always and more.	לְעוֹלָם וָעֶד	7.
ADONAI gives strength to God's People	יי עֹז לְעַמּוֹ יִתֵּן	8.
ADONAI blesses God's People with peace.	יי יְבָרֵךְ אֶת־עַמּוֹ בַשָּׁלוֹם.	9.
Merciful Parent,	אַב הָרַחֲמִים	10.
do GOOD, care about ZION—	הֵיטִיבָה בִרְצוֹנְךָ אֶת־צִיּוֹן	11.
rebuild the walls of JERUSALEM	תִּבְנֶה חוֹמוֹת יְרוּשָׁלָיִם	12.
because in You ALONE do we TRUST	כִּי בְךָ לְבַד בָּטָחְנוּ	13.
Ruler, high and exalted God, Master of Eternity (Masekhet Sofrim).	מֶלֶךְ אֵל רָם וְנִשָּׂא אֲדוֹן עוֹלָמִים.	14.

Commentary

The prayers said before taking the Torah out of the ark are called פְּסוּקִים שֶׁל גְּדֻלָּה, sentences of greatness. They begin our relationship with the Torah by mentioning "great things" about God. (1) Why are "great things about God" the best way to take out the Torah? (2) What is on the top of your "great things about God" list?

The second part of the opening, אַב הָרַחֲמִים, talks about "rebuilding the walls of Jerusalem." Jerusalem is an exciting, vibrant city today. What do we mean when we ask God to "rebuild its walls"?

אֵין means "there is none."

Practice these phrases with the word אֵין .

1. אֵין כָּמוֹךָ בָאֱלֹהִים אֲדֹנָי וְאֵין כְּמַעֲשֶׂיךָ

2. אָבִינוּ מַלְכֵּנוּ אֵין לָנוּ מֶלֶךְ אֶלָּא אָתָּה

3. אֵין לוֹ דְמוּת הַגּוּף וְאֵינוֹ גוּף לֹא נַעֲרֹךְ אֵלָיו קְדֻשָּׁתוֹ

4. אֵין כְּעֶרְכְּךָ וְאֵין זוּלָתֶךָ אֶפֶס בִּלְתֶּךָ וּמִי דוֹמֶה לָךְ

5. הוּא אֱלֹהֵינוּ אֵין עוֹד אֱמֶת מַלְכֵּנוּ אֶפֶס זוּלָתוֹ

6. כִּי הוּא יי אֱלֹהֵינוּ וְאֵין זוּלָתוֹ וַאֲנַחְנוּ יִשְׂרָאֵל עַמּוֹ

7. אֵין כֵּאלֹהֵינוּ אֵין כַּאדוֹנֵנוּ אֵין כְּמַלְכֵּנוּ אֵין כְּמוֹשִׁיעֵנוּ

8. אֵין אַדִּיר כַּיי, אֵין בָּרוּךְ כְּבֶן עַמְרָם, אֵין גְּדֻלָּה כַּתּוֹרָה אֵין דּוֹרְשֶׁיהָ כְּיִשְׂרָאֵל

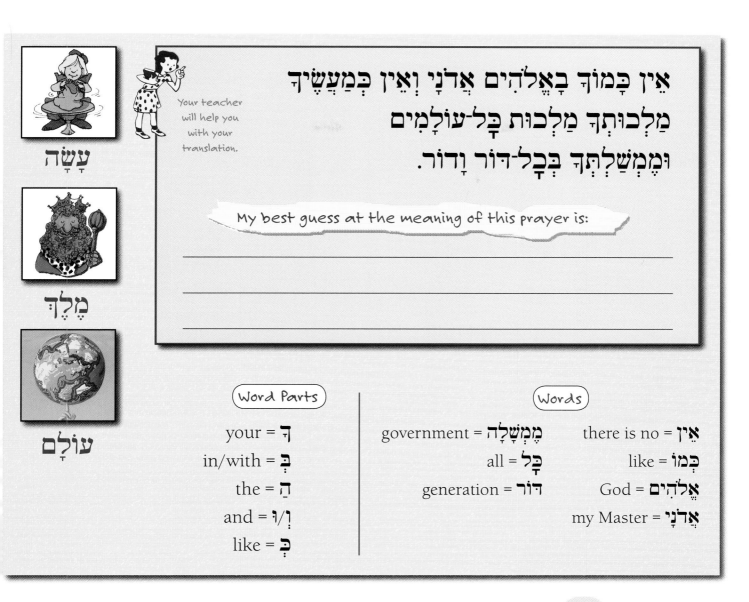

אֵין כָּמוֹךָ בָאֱלֹהִים אֲדֹנָי וְאֵין כְּמַעֲשֶׂיךָ מַלְכוּתְךָ מַלְכוּת כָּל־עוֹלָמִים וּמֶמְשַׁלְתְּךָ בְּכָל־דֹּור וָדֹור.

עֹשֶׂה

מֶלֶךְ

עוֹלָם

My best guess at the meaning of this prayer is:

_____

_____

_____

Word Parts

your = ךָ
in/with = בְּ
the = הַ
and = וְ/וּ
like = כְּ

Words

there is no = אֵין
like = כְּמוֹ
God = אֱלֹהִים
my Master = אֲדֹנָי

government = מֶמְשָׁלָה
all = כָּל
generation = דֹּור

Choreography

In some traditions one stands when beginning אֵין כָּמוֹךָ; in some others one waits until the ark is opened at וַיְהִי בִּנְסֹעַ הָאָרֹן.

Why do we stand when we take out the Torah? Rabbi Abbahu said, "Because the Torah teaches us the words that God said to Moses at Mt. Sinai, 'Stand here with Me and I will tell you all the commandments and laws'" (Deut. 5.25). When we take out the Torah it is as if the Holy One is standing with us (Megillah 21a).

Question: What do we have to do with our heart and our mind to have God standing with us during the Torah service?

Can you see the three letters מלך in these words?

יִמְלֹךְ   מָלַךְ   מֶלֶךְ

Ruler = מֶלֶךְ

ruled = מָלַךְ

will rule = יִמְלֹךְ

Practice these phrases and circle all the words that contain the root מלך.

1. יי מֶלֶךְ יי מָלַךְ יי יִמְלֹךְ לְעוֹלָם וָעֶד   2. לִפְנֵי מֶלֶךְ מַלְכֵי הַמְּלָכִים

3. מַלְכוּתְךָ מַלְכוּת כָּל־עוֹלָמִים וּמֶמְשַׁלְתְּךָ בְּכָל־דּוֹר וָדוֹר

Words

strength = עֹז

nation = עַם

gave = נָתַן

Word Parts

and = וְ/וּ

His/his = וֹ

in/with = בְּ

שָׁלוֹם   בָּרוּךְ   עוֹלָם   מֶלֶךְ

Your teacher will help you with your translation.

יי מֶלֶךְ יי מָלַךְ יי יִמְלֹךְ לְעוֹלָם וָעֶד

יי עֹז לְעַמּוֹ יִתֵּן, יי יְבָרֵךְ אֶת־עַמּוֹ בַשָּׁלוֹם

My best guess at the meaning of this prayer is:

_____

_____

_____

13

The Shepherd's Song

Every night King David would hang his harp over his bed. In the middle of the night the north wind would begin to blow. The wind would move the strings. Slowly a melody would emerge. When that happened, David would wake up and sing with his harp. He would add words and create his psalms. These were David's prayers.

Rabbi Zusya was a Hasidic rabbi who lived in the 1700s. Once he was taking a walk in the country. He heard a shepherd playing a tune on a reed flute. He began to sing along. The melody grabbed him. He sang it to himself over and over. He sang it as he continued his walk. Suddenly he realized that this melody was a long-lost song of King David. At this moment, David's prayer song was returned.

(Martin Buber, *Tales of the Hasidim, Early Masters*)

Questions

1. What do you think is the meaning (message) of this story?
2. The word "revelation" is used to describe a moment when a person comes to hear God's message. Where is the revelation in this story?
3. The Torah service is supposed to be a moment when we experience revelation. Based on this story, how does the Torah service work? How is it a new revelation?

אֵין כָּמוֹךָ .vs מִי כָמֹכָה

Compare these two prayers. What lines have similar words?

1. מִי כָמֹכָה בָּאֵלִים יי	1. אֵין כָּמוֹךָ בָאֱלֹהִים אֲדֹנָי
2. מִי כָמֹכָה נֶאְדָּר בַּקֹּדֶשׁ	2. וְאֵין כְּמַעֲשֶׂיךָ
3. נוֹרָא תְהִלֹּת עֹשֵׂה פֶלֶא.	3. מַלְכוּתְךָ מַלְכוּת כָּל-עוֹלָמִים
4. מַלְכוּתְךָ רָאוּ בָנֶיךָ	4. וּמֶמְשַׁלְתְּךָ בְּכָל-דּוֹר וָדוֹר.
5. בּוֹקֵעַ יָם לִפְנֵי משֶׁה	5. יי מֶלֶךְ יי מָלָךְ
6. זֶה אֵלִי עָנוּ וְאָמְרוּ	6. יי יִמְלֹךְ לְעוֹלָם וָעֶד
7. יי יִמְלֹךְ לְעוֹלָם וָעֶד	7. יי עֹז לְעַמּוֹ יִתֵּן
8. וְנֶאֱמַר כִּי פָדָה יי אֶת-יַעֲקֹב	8. יי יְבָרֵךְ אֶת עַמּוֹ בַשָּׁלוֹם
9. וּגְאָלוֹ מִיַּד חָזָק מִמֶּנּוּ	
10. בָּרוּךְ אַתָּה יי גָּאַל יִשְׂרָאֵל.	

עֲצֹר!

15

Can you see the three letters רצה in these words?

רוֹצֶה   רָצוֹן   תִּרְצוּ

רוֹצֶה = want

רָצוֹן = will/desire

תִּרְצוּ = you will want

Practice these phrases and circle all the words that contain the root רצה.

1. יִהְיוּ לְרָצוֹן אִמְרֵי-פִי וְהֶגְיוֹן לִבִּי לְפָנֶיךָ יי צוּרִי וְגוֹאֲלִי

2. וְהַנְחִילֵנוּ יי אֱלֹהֵינוּ בְּאַהֲבָה וּבְרָצוֹן שַׁבַּת קָדְשֶׁךָ

3. אֲשֶׁר בָּחַר בִּנְבִיאִים טוֹבִים וְרָצָה בְדִבְרֵיהֶם הַנֶּאֱמָרִים בֶּאֱמֶת

4. אַב הָרַחֲמִים הֵיטִיבָה בִרְצוֹנְךָ אֶת-צִיּוֹן תִּבְנֶה חוֹמוֹת יְרוּשָׁלָיִם

5. אִם תִּרְצוּ אֵין זוֹ אַגָּדָה לִהְיוֹת עַם חָפְשִׁי בְּאַרְצֵנוּ אֶרֶץ צִיּוֹן וִירוּשָׁלָיִם

The Meaning of צִיּוֹן

צִיּוֹן is another way of saying Jerusalem. The first time it is used in the Bible is in 2 Samuel 5.7, which says, "Nevertheless David took the fort of צִיּוֹן, that is also known as the city of David." No one knows for sure what צִיּוֹן means. Theories include a rock, a fortress, a dry place, or running water. The name צִיּוֹן was first used for the Jebusite fortress ("the stronghold of צִיּוֹן"), in the southeast of Jerusalem, below the Temple Mount. On its capture by David it was renamed "City of David." In poetry צִיּוֹן is another way of saying Jerusalem. Sometimes it also stands for Judea or the Temple Mount. Later on another part of Jerusalem was labeled as הַר צִיּוֹן, Mt. Zion.

16

Conquer Jerusalem

Conquer Jerusalem by reading from the bottom to the top of this Jerusalem wall.

לְעוֹלָם   חוֹמוֹת   אֲדֹנָי   יְרוּשָׁלַיִם

יִתֵּן   לְעַמּוֹ   וְאֵין   מַלְכוּת

וָדוֹר   מֶלֶךְ   בְּכָל   דוֹר   עֹז

יִמְלֹךְ   וְנִשָּׂא   מֶלֶךְ   יְבָרֵךְ   אֵין

תִּבְנֶה   צִיּוֹן   כָּמוֹךָ   בְּשָׁלוֹם   לְבַד

בָּטַחְנוּ   מַלְכוּתְךָ   כְּמַעֲשֶׂיךָ   בִּרְצוֹנְךָ

בֵּאלֹהִים   עוֹלָמִים   הָרַחֲמִים

וּמֶמְשַׁלְתְּךָ   בִּרְצוֹנְךָ   הֵיטִיבָה

Start Here

חוֹמָה בָּנָה רָצָה טוֹב אָב

יְרוּשָׁלַיִם

אַב הָרַחֲמִים הֵיטִיבָה בִרְצוֹנְךָ אֶת-צִיּוֹן
תִּבְנֶה חוֹמוֹת יְרוּשָׁלָיִם

Your teacher will help you with your translation.

My best guess at the meaning of this prayer is:

_____

_____

_____

Words

mercy = רַחֲמִים

Zion = צִיּוֹן

Word Parts

your = ךָ   the = הַ

in/with = בְּ

To Talk About

The *Tosafot* were French and German biblical commentators, Rashi's descendants and their students. They lived between 1000 and 1300 C.E. They asked the question, "Why is there a special connection between Jerusalem and Torah?" Here is their answer:

Why Jerusalem? The environment of Jerusalem particularly supported Torah study—it was like something in the air. When people saw the holiness of the Temple and the kind of holy work the *Kohanim* did, they were inspired to point their hearts toward the awe of God and the study of Torah.

Questions:

1. What did the *Tosafot* imagine made Jerusalem a special place to study Torah between 160 B.C.E. and 70 C.E.?
2. What things make Jerusalem a special place to study Torah today?

The Walls of Jerusalem

The year was either 1539 or 1540. Suleiman the Magnificent, the sultan, had a palace in Jerusalem. He was looking out one of its many windows and saw an old woman climb up on a hill and dump out a sack of garbage. He was angry to think that some poor woman wanted to turn his neighborhood into a garbage heap. He sent his soldiers to arrest her.

When she was brought into the palace she told Suleiman, "I am sorry, Your Grace, but I am carrying out the commandment of my ancestors." When the sultan questioned her further, she explained, "I am a descendant of the Romans who conquered and destroyed Jerusalem in the year 70. While they destroyed the city, they were unable to destroy the foundations of the Jewish Temple. My ancestors therefore commanded that all Romans in the city had to dump garbage daily on the site where that Temple used to be. Everyone who lived outside the city had to dump garbage there twice a week. And anyone who lived farther than three days away from Jerusalem had to bring garbage to the site at least once a month. When my ancestors couldn't destroy the foundations of the Temple, they decided to make sure that it would always be buried in filth and street mud, to make it a place where no one would want to be. They ordered us to continue to dump garbage on this site so that the Jewish Temple would soon be forgotten."

After hearing this story the sultan ordered his men to arrest anyone else who tried to dump garbage there. Over the next few weeks, several people were arrested every day. Each of them told the same story. Each was bringing garbage to this site because it was a family tradition to make sure that no one remembered the place.

The sultan then issued a royal edict that said, "People who want to find favor in my eyes should come to this location and do the things they see me do." The king then went to the site with a sack of money, a basket, and a broom. First, while he was alone, he threw silver and gold coins all over the mound. Then he began to pick up the big pieces of garbage and put them in his basket. By the time he got to sweeping one small part of the hill, lots of people had joined him. Some of them came to look for gold and silver coins. Others came because they wanted to make the sultan happy. Soon the hill was covered with people sweeping and shoveling, picking up and cleaning. It took more than a month. Every day the sultan came

and worked with them. Every night he seeded the site with a few more coins. When the work was done, the foundations of the Temple could be seen, and a wall, the one we now call the Western Wall, was uncovered.

The sultan issued another royal edict. This one made it a huge crime to litter or even spit in this area.

Next the sultan invited the Jewish community to come and rebuild their Holy Temple at his expense. They politely refused him, saying, "We are not allowed to rebuild God's House until the world is ready. We cannot do it until we have a world where everyone lives in peace." When they said no, the sultan informed them that he would build his own place of prayer nearby. He explained, "I know that your God's house will be a place of prayer for all people. God will listen to people who pray there." The sultan made sure that there was freedom and respect for all Jews who lived in the Ottoman Empire. Last, Suleiman built a wall around Jerusalem to protect Her.

M.M. Reischer, *Sha'arei Yerushalayim*, No. 10, pp 42-3

Questions
1. Why did the sultan choose to uncover the foundations of the Temple?
2. Why wouldn't the Jews accept his offer to rebuild the Temple?
3. Today there are walls around the outside of the Old City of Jerusalem. Today there is a whole modern city of Jerusalem. What are we praying for when we ask God to rebuild the walls of Jerusalem?

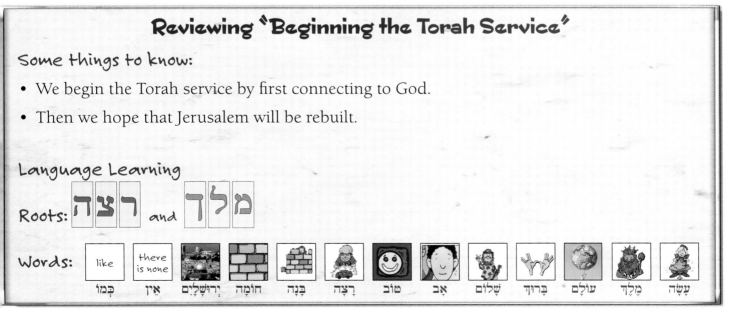

Reviewing "Beginning the Torah Service"

Some things to know:
- We begin the Torah service by first connecting to God.
- Then we hope that Jerusalem will be rebuilt.

Language Learning

Roots: רצה and מלך

Words: כְּמוֹ (like) | אֵין (there is none) | יְרוּשָׁלַיִם | חוֹמָה | בָּנָה | רָצָה | טוֹב | אָב | שָׁלוֹם | בָּרוּךְ | עוֹלָם | מֶלֶךְ | עָשָׂה

Unit 3

The Ark is Opened

When we open the ark, we begin by remembering two moments in Jewish history.

Carrying the Ark

The first moment we act out comes from the time when Israel spent forty years in the wilderness. Every time they moved their camp, the Families-of-Israel were led by the Ark of the Covenant. The Ark followed a pillar of fire at night and a pillar of clouds by day. It was a wooden box, covered inside and out in gold, with winged *cherubim* on top. It was carried on long poles by the *Kohanim* (priests). Inside were (a) the two tablets of the Ten Commandments, (b) the broken fragments of the first set of the Commandments, (c) a jar with a sample of manna, and (d) a copy of the תּוֹרָה scroll. Today, in our synagogue, we still keep the סֵפֶר תּוֹרָה in an ark.

In the Book of Numbers there is a two-sentence-long passage that is surrounded, as if by parentheses, by a pair of upside-down versions of the Hebrew letter נ (*Numbers 10.35-6*). One sentence talks about picking the Ark up. The other sentence talks about putting it down. The first sentence is used at the beginning of the Torah service. The second is used when we return the סֵפֶר תּוֹרָה to the ark. When we take the תּוֹרָה out and when we carry it around the synagogue we are like the Families-of-Israel being led by God through the wilderness.

Jerusalem

The second moment comes from a vision about the future shared by the prophets Isaiah and Micah. They both saw Jerusalem as a center from which the wisdom of Torah would be distributed around the world. The second part of opening the ark involves remembering their dream. Just before we take the Torah out of the ark and begin to make it our own, we share the hope that all people will join in its dream of peace and freedom, justice and kindness. When we take the Torah out of the ark we accept that hope for the future. It comes with the words כִּי מִצִּיּוֹן תֵּצֵא תוֹרָה וּדְבַר יי מִירוּשָׁלָיִם.

(Isaiah 2.3, Micah 4.2)

In this unit you will learn:
• 3 Prayers
• Roots: דבר יצא and
• About the Ark

21

The Ark is Opened

When the Ark was moved	וַיְהִי בִּנְסֹעַ הָאָרֹן .1
Moses would say,	וַיֹּאמֶר מֹשֶׁה .2
Get up, ADONAI,	קוּמָה יי .3
Scatter Your enemies	וְיָפֻצוּ אֹיְבֶיךָ .4
And make those who hate You flee before You (Numbers 10.35).	וְיָנֻסוּ מְשַׂנְאֶיךָ מִפָּנֶיךָ. .5
Because from ZION	כִּי מִצִּיוֹן .6
TORAH will EMERGE	תֵּצֵא תוֹרָה .7
and ADONAI'S WORD (will come)	וּדְבַר יי .8
from JERUSALEM (Isaiah 2.3/Micah 4.2).	מִירוּשָׁלָיִם. .9
BLESSED is the One-Who-GAVE TORAH	בָּרוּךְ שֶׁנָּתַן תּוֹרָה .10
to God's people, ISRAEL, in HOLINESS.	לְעַמּוֹ יִשְׂרָאֵל בִּקְדֻשָּׁתוֹ. .11

Commentary

Rabbi Samson Raphael Hirsch wrote about this part of the Torah service:

"When the Ark is opened we declare, as Moses did when the Ark traveled, that God's word is invincible. Having acknowledged this, we can read from the Torah with proper awareness. We continue that it is God's will that the Torah's message go forth to the entire world, and by blessing God for having given us the Torah, we accept our responsibility to carry out its commands and spread its message."

Questions

1. What part of these prayers were the words that Moses spoke? What does it mean that "God's word is invincible"?
2. How does this truth help us read Torah "with proper awareness"?
3. What part of these prayers says that Torah will go forth to the entire world? Why is this important?
4. What part of the prayer blesses God for the gift of Torah? Why should we spread Torah's message?

Hevruta Study on the Ark of the Covenant

Read these texts with a partner. They all talk about the meaning of the Ark of the Covenant and especially the two כְּרוּבִים (cherubim) that are on top. Explain each text in your own words. Then answer the questions at the bottom together.

THE TORAH: The *cherubim* shall spread out their wings above, covering "the mercy seat" with their wings—each one's face shall look into his brother's... And you shall put the mercy seat on the top of the Ark; and in the Ark you shall put the testimony that I shall give you. There I will meet with you, above the mercy seat and between the two *cherubim* that are upon the Ark of the Testimony. I will speak with you there... (Exodus 25.20-22).

TALMUD: In the Book of Chronicles we are told that "The *cherubim* face toward the Temple," while here we are told that "they face each other." There is no contradiction. When the Jews fulfill God's wishes they "face each other." Each treats the other with politeness and kindness. Each cares about the other. However, when the Jews do not do what God wants, they "face toward the Temple" because they are only concerned about their own holiness and are not concerned about anyone else (*Bava Batra* 99a).

A COMMENTARY: A Jew must have two qualities. Jews must "spread their wings above," always striving to move upward to higher and higher levels, while at the same time "their faces shall look into their brother's/sister's." A Jew must notice another person's distress and always be willing to help. These two qualities are linked to each other (*Sadeh Margalit*).

A COMMENTARY: Said in the name of Danny Landes (with whom I study *Parshat ha-Shavu'ah*), the cherubim are standing "face to face," showing where God can be found: "face to face" in an "I-You" relationship with others (Michael Tolkin).

A COMMENTARY: The *cherubim* were placed by God to guard the entrance to the Garden of Eden when Adam and Eve were kicked out (Genesis 3.24). The *cherubim* kept them from eating from the Tree of Life. These same *cherubim* are placed on the Ark, guarding the Torah scroll inside (Exodus 25.20). We are also told that the Torah can be "a tree of life to them that hold fast to it" (Proverbs 3.18). We learn that the Torah can be our way past the *cherubim* and back to the Garden of Eden (*S'fat Emet*).

Questions

1. What keeps the *cherubim* on top of the Ark from becoming idols like the Golden Calf?
2. What do the *cherubim* teach us about the purpose of the Torah?
3. How does knowing about the Ark of the Covenant help us to point our hearts when we take the Torah out of our ark?

Being Lifted

The Ark

The Ark led the Families-of-Israel through the wilderness. First came a column of smoke or a pillar of fire, then came the Ark, and then came the Families-of-Israel. The Ark used to clear the way for the people. Out of it would come bursts of fire that zapped the scorpions and the snakes out of the way. When God used to talk to Moses, God would speak to him from above the wings of the *cherubim.*

The Ark was very heavy to lift. The Levites would have to struggle with all their might just to lift it a teeny bit above the ground. But once they did that, the Ark took over and carried them (*Numbers Rabbah* 4.20).

The Torah

Rabbi David Moshe Chortkov was a <u>H</u>asidic rabbi. He once had to hold a large, heavy Torah for a long time. One of his students offered to share the weight, but Rabbi David said to him, "Once you've picked up the Torah, it is no longer heavy. It carries you" (Martin Buber, *Tales of the Hasidim*).

The Grandson

November 9, 1938, was Kristallnacht, the "Night of Broken Glass." Gangs of Nazi youth roamed through Jewish neighborhoods breaking windows of Jewish businesses and homes, burning synagogues and looting. One hundred and one synagogues and almost seventy-five hundred Jewish businesses were destroyed. Twenty-six thousand Jews were arrested and sent to concentration camps. Jews were physically attacked and beaten, and ninety-one died (Louis L Snyder, *Encyclopedia of the Third Reich*).

It was just before sundown, and the burning and the breaking had started. A Jewish grandfather and his son were too far away from home. Around them gangs of youth, whipped into craziness by the Nazi machine, were throwing rocks. The grandfather took the young boy's hand. He began to walk more quickly. He looked behind and saw that they were being followed. They broke into a run. The boy fell, hurt his knee, and started to cry. The grandfather threw down his cane, scooped up the boy, and continued running. The gangs were closing in on them. Out of a window people called to him, "Put the boy down. You need all your own strength. The boy can run faster than you." The grandfather called back, "I am not carrying him—he is lifting me up" (Morris Silverman, *Heaven on Your Head: Interpretations and Legends of the Torah and Holidays*).

Questions

1. What do these three stories have in common?
2. How are people "lifted up and carried" by the Ark, the Torah, and a child in their arms?
3. How do these stories help us know where to point our hearts when we take the Torah out of the ark?

Can you see the root יצא in these words?

Sometimes the ' drops out.

הַמּוֹצִיא   בְּצֵאת   יָצָא

left = יָצָא

when leaving = בְּצֵאת

the One Who takes out = הַמּוֹצִיא

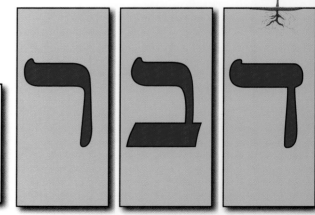

Practice these phrases and circle all the words that contain the root יצא.

2. כִּי מִצִּיּוֹן תֵּצֵא תוֹרָה וּדְבַר יי מִירוּשָׁלָיִם	1. בְּצֵאת יִשְׂרָאֵל מִמִּצְרָיִם
4. אֲשֶׁר הוֹצֵאתִי אֶתְכֶם מֵאֶרֶץ מִצְרָיִם	3. הַמּוֹצִיא לֶחֶם מִן הָאָרֶץ

Can you see the root דבר in these words?

עֲשֶׂרֶת הַדִּבְּרוֹת   וְדִבַּרְתָּ   דָּבָר

word/thing = דָּבָר

and you will speak = וְדִבַּרְתָּ

עֲשֶׂרֶת הַדִּבְּרוֹת =
the Ten Commandments

Practice these phrases and circle all the words that contain the root דבר.

6. וְשִׁנַּנְתָּם לְבָנֶיךָ וְדִבַּרְתָּ בָּם	5. וּדְבַר יי מִירוּשָׁלָיִם
8. וְדָבָר אֶחָד מִדְּבָרֶיךָ אָחוֹר לֹא יָשׁוּב רֵיקָם	7. אֵלּוּ דְבָרִים שֶׁאֵין לָהֶם שִׁעוּר
10. הַמְדַבֵּר וּמְקַיֵּם שֶׁכָּל־דְּבָרָיו אֱמֶת וָצֶדֶק	9. הָאֵל הַנֶּאֱמָן בְּכָל־דְּבָרָיו

25

Your teacher will help you with your translation.

כִּי מִצִּיּוֹן תֵּצֵא תוֹרָה וּדְבַר יי מִירוּשָׁלָיִם

My best guess at the meaning of this prayer is:

_____

_____

_____

Commentary

Rabbi Naḥman of Bretzlav was a Ḥasidic teacher who lived around the same time as Abraham Lincoln. He looked at the verse about Torah coming from Jerusalem and then taught this lesson.

Real enlightenment and wisdom happen only in the Land of Israel. But even the People of Israel outside the Land have the power to draw enlightenment and wisdom from there. Every single Jew has a share in the Land. Using their share, Jews draw wisdom from the Land. But those who insult the honor of the Almighty are cut off from the light that comes from the Land of Israel, and they fall into the mentality of "outside the Land" that is one of conflict and divisiveness (*Likutey Moharan II, 71*).

Questions

1. How can the Land of Israel teach people? How can it be "enlightenment" to people who are not there?
2. What do you think it means to be "cut off from the light that comes from the Land of Israel"? How do you think being cut off from the Land leads to fighting?
3. How can thinking about Israel help to put you in the right frame of mind to take out the תּוֹרָה?

26

The Torah Service

1. אֵין כָּמוֹךָ בָאֱלֹהִים אֲדֹנָי וְאֵין כְּמַעֲשֶׂיךָ

2. מַלְכוּתְךָ מַלְכוּת כָּל־עוֹלָמִים וּמֶמְשַׁלְתְּךָ בְּכָל־דּוֹר וָדֹר

3. יְיָ מֶלֶךְ יְיָ מָלָךְ יְיָ יִמְלֹךְ לְעוֹלָם וָעֶד

4. יְיָ עֹז לְעַמּוֹ יִתֵּן יְיָ יְבָרֵךְ אֶת־עַמּוֹ בַשָּׁלוֹם

5. אַב הָרַחֲמִים הֵיטִיבָה בִרְצוֹנְךָ אֶת־צִיּוֹן תִּבְנֶה חוֹמוֹת יְרוּשָׁלָיִם

6. כִּי בְךָ לְבַד בָּטָחְנוּ מֶלֶךְ אֵל רָם וְנִשָּׂא אֲדוֹן עוֹלָמִים

7. וַיְהִי בִּנְסֹעַ הָאָרֹן וַיֹּאמֶר מֹשֶׁה

8. קוּמָה יְיָ וְיָפֻצוּ אֹיְבֶיךָ וְיָנֻסוּ מְשַׂנְאֶיךָ מִפָּנֶיךָ

9. כִּי מִצִּיּוֹן תֵּצֵא תוֹרָה וּדְבַר יְיָ מִירוּשָׁלָיִם

10. בָּרוּךְ שֶׁנָּתַן תּוֹרָה לְעַמּוֹ יִשְׂרָאֵל בִּקְדֻשָּׁתוֹ

11. אֶחָד אֱלֹהֵינוּ גָּדוֹל אֲדוֹנֵינוּ קָדוֹשׁ שְׁמוֹ

12. גַּדְּלוּ לַיְיָ אִתִּי וּנְרוֹמְמָה שְׁמוֹ יַחְדָּו

The Last Kopeck

In a little village called Shmunefka the impossible happened. There was not a single kopeck left in the village. In fact there was no money of any kind. Even if you offered someone a ruble for a kopeck, they would be unable to give you one. People came running to the rabbi and asked, "What should we do?" The rabbi washed his hands and said שֶׁהֶחֱיָנוּ over something new.

Still, the panic went on, so the rabbi called a meeting. People gathered at the synagogue and waited for the rabbi to speak. He ascended the בִּימָה and said, "Jews, it will do us no good to get angry at God. Everything that God does is either because of זְכוּת אָבוֹת וְאִמָּהוֹת, the merit of our ancestors, or for the coming of the messiah. While it is hard to believe that our little town is so important, the lack of money here assures the coming of the messiah. In the Talmud we are taught 'The seed of David will not come until no Jew has a single coin in his pocket.' That time is now, and that place is here."

Reb Ḥayyim said, "But what about the Zionists and all their settlements in אֶרֶץ יִשְׂרָאֵל? Do they have nothing to do with the messiah?"

The rabbi answered, "Prepare for your journey to Zion. When the messiah comes we will all return there. The pioneers have prepared our path."

The joyful mood was interrupted by Menaḥem Mendel, the contractor. He said, "I have been going over the accounts for the building of the new public baths, and one kopeck is left over." He pulled out a ream of papers and found a small envelope with one kopeck in it. He put the coin down on the table and said, "This belongs to the community." Everyone looked at it as if it were the first coin in the world.

Shmuel yelled at him, "Go and check your records. Last month you told us we were one hundred and thirty-eight rubles short—now you say we are one kopeck over. Check your records."

The rabbi said, "The records do not matter. The messiah cannot come because we have a coin here."

One person said, "Throw the coin into the river. It will be gone, and the messiah will come."

Another person said, "Not into the river. It is a mitzvah never to destroy anything useful. Besides, a fish might swallow it, and someone would catch it and we would have the coin back. We should throw it into the public baths. There is so much mud on its floor that no one will ever find it there."

David, the principal of the Talmud Torah, said, "The roof of the Talmud Torah, the school, leaks. We should assign the kopek to repair the roof of the school. That would be using it to do a mitzvah."

Barukh, the shamas, said, "No, not the Talmud Torah! When the messiah comes we will not use it anymore. We should use it to repair the synagogue that also leaks. It is more of an embarrassment to have a leaky synagogue."

Mr. Kaufman, head of the Shmunefka burial society, argued, "The synagogue is holy, but what about a cemetery? When the messiah comes we will take the holy things out of the synagogue and take them to Jerusalem with us. When he comes the synagogue will be only the four walls—but the cemetery will be here. We need to protect the cemetery from all the animals breaking in and walking through. It needs a new fence."

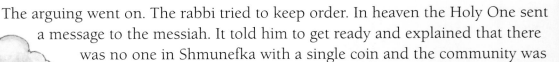

The arguing went on. The rabbi tried to keep order. In heaven the Holy One sent a message to the messiah. It told him to get ready and explained that there was no one in Shmunefka with a single coin and the community was having a meeting to get rid of the one communal kopeck. "Jewish communities," the message explained, "are good at spending money."

The messiah sent for his white donkey and his shofar. Both had been sitting and waiting for hundreds of years. The donkey was covered in dust and had to be washed twice; the shofar had to be soaked in vinegar for hours. Finally they were ready, and the messiah mounted the donkey and flew to Shmunefka. He said the words of the Psalm 126, "When the Eternal brought us back to Zion we were like dreamers." On his face was a huge smile.

As he came into the town the meeting was ending. The Jews of the town were screaming and fighting. "For the cemetery." "No. For the school." "Throw it away." There was kicking and screaming. Everyone was angry. The messiah said quietly, "No, I have come too soon" *(based on a story by Shimon Frug).*

Questions

1. When he was so close, what kept the messiah from coming?
2. This story is about a small village called Shmunefka. What does it teach us about "the Torah coming from Jerusalem"?
3. In what ways does the Torah come from Jerusalem today? In what ways does the Torah still need to come from Jerusalem?
4. How does knowing this story help us know where to point our hearts when we sing כִּי מִצִּיּוֹן?

Reviewing "The Ark is Opened"

Some things to know:

• When we open the ark in the synagogue we recall the Ark that led Israel in the wilderness.

• We also connect to the image of the Torah spreading from Jerusalem.

Language Learning

Roots: and

Words:
יְרוּשָׁלַיִם   תּוֹרָה   דָּבָר   יָצָא

A Key Phrase:

כִּי מִצִּיּוֹן תֵּצֵא תוֹרָה וּדְבַר יי מִירוּשָׁלָיִם

30

Taking the Torah out of the Ark

Between the time we open the ark and the time we take the Torah out of the ark, some communities use this moment to say a few prayers. Some of these are said only on holidays, while others are said every Shabbat.

שְׁמַע

The **שְׁמַע** makes the moment when we take the Torah out of the ark feel like the moment when Israel stood at Mt. Sinai. According to a midrash, the Families-of-Israel were all standing at the foot of Mt. Sinai, and Moses led them in the **שְׁמַע** when God spoke words of Torah to them (*Deuteronomy Rabbah 2.31*). We do the same today. It was the moment when Israel said, "**נַעֲשֶׂה וְנִשְׁמַע**. WE WILL DO, AND WE WILL OBEY" (Exodus 24.7).

אֶחָד אֱלֹהֵינוּ

Next comes a sentence that is not in the Bible. **אֶחָד אֱלֹהֵינוּ** is found in a book called *Masekhet Sofrim* that is not part of the Talmud but is often found with it. It gives lots of rules about the Torah. This verse is an echo of the **שְׁמַע**. It is made up of biblical phrases (*Psalm 147.5, Isaiah 57.15*).

גַּדְּלוּ לַיי אִתִּי

The third verse in the taking out of the Torah comes from Psalm 34.4. It tells a story. In Hebrew **גַּדְּלוּ** is made up of six words. In II Samuel 6.13 we learn that when David brought the Ark up to Jerusalem he stopped and had a celebration every six steps. The **שְׁמַע** has us receiving the Torah with Moses; **גַּדְּלוּ** has us bringing the Ark with the Torah up to Jerusalem.

לְךָ יי

With **לְךָ יי** the Torah processional begins. The **לְךָ יי** is made up of two verses from two different places. The first comes from the story where David announces that his son Solomon will be building the Temple (*I Chronicles 29.11*). We begin by following the Ark into Solomon's Temple, its home. The second verse comes from Psalms. It was written by David, and it praises the establishment of the Temple Mount as a Holy Place of Torah (*Psalm 99.5, 9*). The celebration continues.

In this unit you will learn:
• 4 Prayers
• Roots: **רום, שחה, גדל, שמע**
• That taking the Torah out of the ark is like being at Mt. Sinai and like bringing the Ark up to Jerusalem.

31

Taking the Torah Out of the Ark

English	Hebrew	#
LISTEN, Israel	שְׁמַע יִשְׂרָאֵל	1.
ADONAI is our God	יי אֱלֹהֵינוּ	2.
ADONAI is ONE (Deuteronomy 6.4).	יי אֶחָד.	4.
Our God is ONE	אֶחָד אֱלֹהֵינוּ	5.
BIG is our Master	גָּדוֹל אֲדוֹנֵינוּ	6.
HOLY is God's Name (Masekhet Sofrim 14.8).	קָדוֹשׁ שְׁמוֹ.	7.
EXPAND Adonai together with me (Psalm 34.4)	גַּדְּלוּ לַיי אִתִּי	8.
And let us ELEVATE God's Name TOGETHER.	וּנְרוֹמְמָה שְׁמוֹ יַחְדָּו.	9.
ADONAI, You have:	לְךָ יי	10.
the GREATNESS, the POWER, the GLORY,	הַגְּדֻלָּה וְהַגְּבוּרָה וְהַתִּפְאֶרֶת	11.
the VICTORY, and the MAJESTY.	וְהַנֵּצַח וְהַהוֹד	12.
Everything that is in HEAVEN and EARTH is Yours, ADONAI	כִּי כֹל בַּשָּׁמַיִם וּבָאָרֶץ לְךָ יי	13.
SOVEREIGNTY and LEADERSHIP	הַמַּמְלָכָה וְהַמִּתְנַשֵּׂא	14.
above all heads of state—are Yours (I Chronicles 29.11).	לְכֹל לְרֹאשׁ.	15.
LIFT UP ADONAI our God	רוֹמְמוּ יי אֱלֹהֵינוּ	16.
and bow down to God's footstool (Psalm 99.5).	וְהִשְׁתַּחֲווּ לַהֲדֹם רַגְלָיו.	17.
God is HOLY.	קָדוֹשׁ הוּא.	18.
LIFT UP ADONAI our God	רוֹמְמוּ יי אֱלֹהֵינוּ	19.
and bow down to God's HOLY mountain	וְהִשְׁתַּחֲווּ לְהַר קָדְשׁוֹ	20.
because ADONAI—our God—is HOLY (Psalm 99.9).	כִּי קָדוֹשׁ יי אֱלֹהֵינוּ.	21.

Mishnah: When three persons have eaten together, it is their duty to invite one another to say *Birkat ha-Mazon*. The invitation is the responsive part at the beginning.

Gemara: Where in the Torah do we learn this mitzvah? Rabbi Assi says, "From the verse 'EXPAND Adonai together with me and let us ELEVATE God's Name TOGETHER'" (Psalm 34.4). Rabbi Abbahu learned from this that "When I (one person) proclaim the name of the Eternal, you (at least two) describe the greatness of our God" (Deuteronomy 32.3) (*Brakhot* 45a).

Question: In what ways are *Birkat ha-Mazon* (Grace after Meals) and taking out the Torah similar things?

Can you see the three letters שמע in these words?

לִשְׁמֹעַ   שְׁמַע   שׁוֹמֵעַ

to listen = לִשְׁמֹעַ

listen! (command) = שְׁמַע

listens = שׁוֹמֵעַ

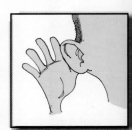

Practice these phrases and circle all the words that contain the root שמע.

1. שְׁמַע יִשְׂרָאֵל יי אֱלֹהֵינוּ יי אֶחָד

2. הַשְׁמִיעֵנוּ אֶל הַמְיֻחָד

3. בָּרוּךְ אַתָּה יי שׁוֹמֵעַ תְּפִלָּה

4. אָבִינוּ מַלְכֵּנוּ שְׁמַע קוֹלֵנוּ

Can you see the root גדל in these words?

גָּדוֹל   גַּדְּלוּ   יִתְגַּדַּל

big = גָּדוֹל

expand = גַּדְּלוּ

magnified = יִתְגַּדַּל

Practice these phrases and circle all the words that contain the root גדל.

5. גַּדְּלוּ לַיי אִתִּי וּנְרוֹמְמָה שְׁמוֹ יַחְדָּו

6. הָאֵל הַגָּדוֹל הַגִּבּוֹר וְהַנּוֹרָא

7. יְגַדֵּל אֱלֹהִים חַי וְיִשְׁתַּבַּח

8. יִתְגַּדַּל וְיִתְקַדַּשׁ שְׁמֵהּ רַבָּא

9. גָּדוֹל יי וּמְהֻלָּל מְאֹד וְלִגְדֻלָּתוֹ אֵין חֵקֶר

10. הִגְדִּיל יי לַעֲשׂוֹת עִמָּנוּ

33

קָדוֹשׁ  גָּדוֹל אֶחָד יִשְׂרָאֵל שְׁמַע

Words

God's name = יי

our God = אֱלֹהֵינוּ

master = אָדוֹן

His name = שְׁמוֹ

with me = אִתִּי

lift up = רוֹם

together = יַחַד

Word Parts

our = ◼נוּ

his = ◼וֹ

to/for = לְ

Your teacher will help you with your translation.

שְׁמַע יִשְׂרָאֵל יי אֱלֹהֵינוּ יי אֶחָד

אֶחָד אֱלֹהֵינוּ גָּדוֹל אֲדוֹנֵינוּ קָדוֹשׁ שְׁמוֹ

גַּדְּלוּ לַיי אִתִּי וּנְרוֹמְמָה שְׁמוֹ יַחְדָּו

My best guess at the meaning of this prayer is:

_____

_____

_____

To Talk About

Why was Israel considered holy enough to recite the שְׁמַע? Rabbi Pinḥas ben Hama told this story: "Israel earned the right to recite the שְׁמַע on Mt. Sinai. God first began to speak to them at Mt. Sinai by saying, שְׁמַע יִשְׂרָאֵל ('Listen Israel'). Then God said, 'I am the Eternal your God.' Israel immediately answered יי אֱלֹהֵינוּ יי אֶחָד ('The Eternal is our God, the Eternal alone'). Then Moses said, 'Blessed be the Name Whose glorious empire is for ever and ever.'"

(*Deuteronomy Rabbah* 2.31)

Questions

1. How does Rabbi Pinḥas' story explain why Israel is given the privilege of saying the שְׁמַע?
2. How is the beginning of the Torah service like being on Mt. Sinai and hearing God teach Torah?
3. Based on this teaching, where should we point our hearts when we say the שְׁמַע during the service for taking out the Torah?

עֲצֹר!

34

Can you see the three letters שחה in these words?

וְהִשְׁתַּחֲוּ   אֶשְׁתַּחֲוֶה   שָׁחָה

שָׁחָה = bow down

אֶשְׁתַּחֲוֶה = I will bow down

וְהִשְׁתַּחֲוּ = and bow down

Practice these phrases and circle all the words that contain the root שחה.

1. וְהִשְׁתַּחֲוּ לְהַר קָדְשׁוֹ

2. וַאֲנַחְנוּ כּוֹרְעִים וּמִשְׁתַּחֲוִים וּמוֹדִים

3. וְהִשְׁתַּחֲוּ לַהֲדֹם רַגְלָיו

4. וַאֲנִי אֶשְׁתַּחֲוֶה וְאֶכְרָעָה אֲבָרְכָה

Can you see the root רום in these words?

רוֹמְמוּ   מָרוֹם   רָם

רָם = high

מָרוֹם = heights

רוֹמְמוּ = elevate

Practice these phrases and circle all the words that contain the root רום.

5. רוֹמְמוּ יי אֱלֹהֵינוּ

6. שׁוֹכֵן עַד מָרוֹם וְקָדוֹשׁ שְׁמוֹ

7. בַּמָּרוֹם יְלַמְּדוּ עֲלֵיהֶם וְעָלֵינוּ

8. רָם וְנִשָּׂא גָּדוֹל וְנוֹרָא

9. אֲרוֹמִמְךָ אֱלֹהַי הַמֶּלֶךְ וַאֲבָרְכָה שִׁמְךָ לְעוֹלָם וָעֶד

35

קָדוֹשׁ

הַר

שָׁחָה

רוֹם

Your teacher will help you with your translation.

רוֹמְמוּ יי אֱלֹהֵינוּ

וְהִשְׁתַּחֲווּ לְהַר קָדְשׁוֹ

כִּי קָדוֹשׁ יי אֱלֹהֵינוּ

My best guess at the meaning of this prayer is:

_____

_____

_____

Choreography

1. The Torah is taken out of the ark by a person who is called the **מוֹצִיא** *motzi*, "the one who takes out." It is handed to the **שְׁלִיחַ צִבּוּר**, "the community representative."

2. The **שְׁלִיחַ צִבּוּר** lifts the Torah slightly and sings the **שְׁמַע**. The congregation repeats this line.

3. The **שְׁלִיחַ צִבּוּר** lifts the Torah a second time and sings **אֶחָד אֱלֹהֵינוּ**. The congregation again echoes this line.

4. The **שְׁלִיחַ צִבּוּר** turns toward the ark, bows and sings **גַּדְּלוּ לַיי אִתִּי**.

5. The congregation responds with **לְךָ יי**, and a **הַקָּפָה**, a Torah procession, around of the synagogue. People come out into the aisles and kiss the Torah by first touching the mantle with a **טַלִּית**, a **סִדּוּר**, or a hand. This object is then touched to the lips. It is as if we are bringing the words of Torah to our lips.

Question: When we bring the Torah around the congregation we act out the closeness and connection we feel to its words. What keeps the Torah from becoming an idol, a thing we worship?

36

The Synagogue That Cried

At the edge of town there is an abandoned synagogue that people call the weeping synagogue. Birds nest there. Squirrels come and play there. But no one prays there. Many of the local Jews believe that it is haunted. They abandoned it, moved the Holy Torah scrolls, turned off the Eternal Light, and built a brand new synagogue on the other side of town. This is the story the oldest members of the community tell about it.

"Once, long ago, we had a rabbi who was a scholar. He taught brilliant classes and gave astounding sermons. Late at night he could often be found alone in the synagogue, the old synagogue, studying the holy books. He would study late into the night and early into the next morning.

"One night, when the rabbi was the last person awake in the whole town, a voice spoke to him from inside the Holy Ark. It said, 'Make a wish. Heaven has seen how good and how holy you are, so make a wish.'

"He thought and thought, then said, 'I have nothing for which to wish. I have health and family. I have enough to eat and wear, enough things, enough of a place to live. I am happy with work. I am happy with my portion in life.'

"At that moment the ark began to cry. A huge sobbing started. Then the voice began to speak again. 'You could have done so much. You could have brought peace or ended hunger. Human suffering could have ended, but you thought of wishes as only for you.' The crying continued.

"In the morning they found the rabbi collapsed on the floor. They woke him, took him home, washed his forehead, and fed him soup. By evening he was gone. He said nothing to anyone. The crying started that day. From that day the synagogue felt like a sad place. At night when the wind blew, it became a

37

sobbing voice that seemed to come from the ark. Anyone who was in the synagogue heard the ark cry, 'If only... If only...'

"It became too much for the community. They built a new synagogue and started over" (*based on a story by David Einhorn*).

Questions

1. What does this story teach us about wishing and praying?
2. Why do most Jewish prayers use the words "we" and "our" and not "my" and "I"?
3. How does this story help us know where to point our hearts when we open up the ark and begin to take the Torah out?
4. It is a Sefardic custom to stand in front of an open ark or especially an open Torah scroll and say a personal prayer. Why is this a good place for praying?

Reviewing "Taking the Torah out of the Ark"

Some things to know

- The Torah service includes references to Mt. Sinai, taking the Torah up to Jerusalem, and the opening of Solomon's Temple.
- This part if the service is described in a book called *Maseket Sofrim*.

Language Learning

Roots:  , ,   and

Words:

קָדוֹשׁ   הַר   שָׁחָה   רוֹם

38

The Torah Blessings

When one is "called" to the Torah one has an "עֲלִיָּה *aliyah*." עֲלִיָּה means "going up." The person receiving an עֲלִיָּה says blessings before and after the reading of the Torah. Originally, and sometimes still, the person who has the עֲלִיָּה also reads his or her portion of the Torah.

Question: What do you think is the "up" in being called to the Torah?

Different synagogues read Torah differently. Traditionally, Torah is read on Monday and Thursday mornings, and twice on Shabbat (morning and afternoon). Today some synagogues read Torah on Friday night. Traditionally there are three עֲלִיּוֹת that connect to each Torah reading. On Shabbat morning the tradition calls for seven עֲלִיּוֹת and a person called the מַפְטִיר who will go on to read the הַפְטָרָה. On Jewish holidays there can be four, five or six עֲלִיּוֹת. Some synagogues read fewer than the traditional number of עֲלִיּוֹת.

We say a blessing both before and after reading Torah. Very few acts in the Jewish tradition get blessings both before and after. We bless before and after eating. We bless both before and after reading תּוֹרָה, הַפְטָרָה, and the Purim Megillah. The Talmud connects eating to the other three. It explains that food nourishes our bodies while תּוֹרָה feeds our souls. Food keeps us alive while תּוֹרָה plants within us eternal life (*Brakhot* 21a).

Question:
How does the תּוֹרָה give us eternal life?

In this unit you will learn:
- בְּרָכוֹת 2
- Root: נ ת ן
- The rituals of reading Torah
- The issue of being "chosen."

The Torah Blessings

Before the Torah Reading

BLESS ADONAI—the One who is BLESSED.	בָּרְכוּ אֶת יי הַמְבֹרָךְ .1
(Yes) BLESSED is ADONAI— the One who is BLESSED forever and beyond.	בָּרוּךְ יי הַמְבֹרָךְ לְעוֹלָם וָעֶד. .2
BLESSED are You, ADONAI	בָּרוּךְ אַתָּה יי .3
OUR God, Ruler of the cosmos	אֱלֹהֵינוּ מֶלֶךְ הָעוֹלָם .4
Who CHOSE US from all the nations	אֲשֶׁר בָּחַר בָּנוּ מִכָּל־הָעַמִּים .5
Who draws us close to Your service.	אֲשֶׁר קֵרְבָנוּ לַעֲבוֹדָתוֹ*
And Who GAVE US the TORAH.	וְנָתַן לָנוּ אֶת־תּוֹרָתוֹ. .6
BLESSED are You, ADONAI, GIVER of the TORAH.	בָּרוּךְ אַתָּה יי נוֹתֵן הַתּוֹרָה. .7

After the Torah Reading

BLESSED are You, ADONAI	בָּרוּךְ אַתָּה יי .8
OUR God, Ruler of the cosmos	אֱלֹהֵינוּ מֶלֶךְ הָעוֹלָם .9
Who GAVE US the TORAH of TRUTH	אֲשֶׁר נָתַן לָנוּ תּוֹרַת אֱמֶת .10
And PLANTED within us ETERNAL LIFE.	וְחַיֵּי עוֹלָם נָטַע בְּתוֹכֵנוּ. .11
BLESSED are You, ADONAI, GIVER of the TORAH.	בָּרוּךְ אַתָּה יי נוֹתֵן הַתּוֹרָה. .12

*from the Reconstructionist Siddur

When a person recites the blessings over the Torah, s/he should point his/her heart to the giving of the Torah and experience the moment when God gave us the Holy Torah that is the source of our life. The Torah is God's cherished possession that gives God delight every day (*Tur, Laws of Morning Blessings*, Ch. 47).

Questions: (1) What about the Torah gives God delight? (2) How can we tap into that?

This blessing first says "Who GAVE US the TORAH" in the past tense. It then calls God "GIVER of the TORAH" (present tense). Zev Wolf of Zhitomir pointed out this change in tense (*Or ha-Meir*, vol 1.8).

Questions: (1) How can the "giving" of the Torah be both past and present tense? (2) What do we have to do to make מַתַּן־תּוֹרָה (the giving of Torah) a present-tense experience? (3) How does this insight help you know where to point your heart when you say the Torah blessings?

Can you see the three letters נתן in these words?

נָתַן   נוֹתֵן   יִתֵּן

gave = נָתַן

gives = נוֹתֵן

will give = יִתֵּן

Practice these phrases and circle all the words that contain the root נתן.

1. אֲשֶׁר נָתַן לָנוּ תּוֹרַת אֱמֶת   2. בָּרוּךְ אַתָּה יי נוֹתֵן הַתּוֹרָה

3. יי עֹז לְעַמּוֹ יִתֵּן   4. שֶׁנָּתַתָּ לָנוּ יי אֱלֹהֵינוּ לְשָׂשׂוֹן וּלְשִׂמְחָה

5. וְנָתַן לָנוּ אֶת־תּוֹרָתוֹ   6. וְאַתָּה נוֹתֵן לָהֶם אֶת־אָכְלָם בְּעִתּוֹ

Choosing/Chosen

The opening Torah blessing centers on the idea that God chose the Jewish people. This is an idea found in the Torah, Midrash and Talmud, but it is also an idea that has made many modern Jews uncomfortable. Here are a number of different ways that different siddurim have dealt with this passage. (A) is the traditional version that is also usually found in Orthodox and Conservative synagogues. (B) is the version found in most Reform synagogues. (C) is the version created by Abraham Geiger, founder of Reform Judaism. (D) is the version created by Mordechai Kaplan, the founder of Reconstructionist Judaism, and it is still the prime version found in Reconstructionist siddurim.

A. אֲשֶׁר בָּחַר בָּנוּ מִכָּל־הָעַמִּים—Who chose us from all the nations (traditional)

B. אֲשֶׁר בָּחַר בָּנוּ מִכָּל־הָעַמִּים—Who called us from all people (Union Prayer Book)

C. אֲשֶׁר בָּחַר בָּנוּ—Who gave us a religious vocation (Abraham Geiger)

D. אֲשֶׁר קֵרְבָנוּ לַעֲבוֹדָתוֹ—Who hast drawn us to Your service (Mordechai Kaplan)

Questions
1. Which Hebrew text is used in your synagogue?
2. Which English understanding is used in your synagogue?
3. Which one would you prefer?

נָתַן

עוֹלָם

מֶלֶךְ

אַתָּה

בָּרוּךְ

תּוֹרָה

Your teacher will help you with your translation.

בָּרוּךְ אַתָּה יי אֱלֹהֵינוּ מֶלֶךְ הָעוֹלָם
אֲשֶׁר בָּחַר בָּנוּ מִכָּל־הָעַמִּים
וְנָתַן לָנוּ אֶת־תּוֹרָתוֹ.
בָּרוּךְ אַתָּה יי נוֹתֵן הַתּוֹרָה.

My best guess at the meaning of this prayer is:

_____

_____

_____

_____

(Words)

אֲשֶׁר = who

בָּחַר = chose

כֹּל = all

עַמִּים = nations

(Word Parts)

בְּ/בָּ = in/with

נוּ■ = us, our

מִ = from

הַ = the

לְ/לָ = to/for

How to have an עֲלִיָה

1. Walk up on the bimah. Shake the appropriate hands.

2. The Torah reader will open the scroll and point to the place where the Torah reading will begin. Take your טַלִית, use a corner to touch that place, and then bring the טַלִית to your lips.

3. Hold each of the Torah rollers in a hand, roll the scroll together, and say the opening בְּרָכָה.

4. Let go with your left hand but continue to hold onto the right roller with your right hand as the Torah is read.

5. When the reading is finished, again take the scroll in both hands, one on each roller, close the scroll, and say the closing בְּרָכָה.

6. Move to the left and wait for the next person to finish his or her עֲלִיָה. When that person is done you can shake hands and return to your seat. On the way many people will shake your hand and say יִישַׁר כֹּחֲךָ or יִישַׁר כֹּחַ (may your strength increase).

Question: Why is a Torah honor called an עֲלִיָה (a going up)?

Ezra's Moment

The Temple was in Jerusalem. It was the one place where all Jews went to connect to God. It was a place of community, prayer, and Torah. In the Temple there were three copies of the Torah. In each there was one mistake. They were the oldest and best copies. These were used to check all other Torah scrolls that were written (*Mesekhet Sofrim* 6.4). The king and the priests used to read Torah to the people in the Temple (*Sotah* 7.7-8). It is probable that in those days the Temple was the only place that a copy of the Torah could be found.

We don't know when local synagogues got started. We suspect that it happened before the first Temple was destroyed and before the Jewish people were exiled to Babylonia. We suspect that the synagogue became more important to the Jewish people during the Babylonian exile. We know that the synagogue remained important once they returned.

One Rosh ha-Shanah after the Jewish people returned from Babylonia, Ezra the scribe gathered the people in the square by the Water Gate. He took a Torah scroll and climbed on a high wooden tower and read Torah to the people. As part of the ceremony he said words that were very much like "בָּרְכוּ אֶת יי הַמְבֹרָךְ." The people then responded in a way that was very much like

"בָּרוּךְ יי הַמְבֹרָךְ לְעוֹלָם וָעֶד" (*Nehemiah* 8). He showed the text to the people in a way that was very much like the way we make הַגְבָּהָה *hagbahah* (lifting up the text to the congregation) today.

Ezra had copies of the Torah written. They were taken to every Jewish community and placed in a synagogue in every village and town. On Monday and Thursday, Ezra had the elders of the town sit in the gates and use the Torah to judge between the people. On Monday, Thursday, and Saturday, Ezra had each community read and teach the Torah in synagogue. This was the moment when the Torah moved out of the Temple and was placed in the hands of every Jew. The Torah was now ours to explain and teach.

We still follow Ezra's ruling and read the Torah weekly in synagogue. When we do, we begin each reading with words very much like those that Ezra used at the Water Gate. We begin "בָּרְכוּ אֶת יי הַמְבֹרָךְ".

Questions

1. What was important about the day that Ezra read Torah to the nation?
2. How have we made our memory of that day part of our Torah service?
3. How does knowing this story help us to point our hearts when we hear or say the Torah blessings?

Torah Service Practice

1. אֵין כָּמוֹךָ בָאֱלֹהִים אֲדֹנָי וְאֵין כְּמַעֲשֶׂיךָ.

2. מַלְכוּתְךָ מַלְכוּת כָּל־עוֹלָמִים וּמֶמְשַׁלְתְּךָ בְּכָל־דּוֹר וָדוֹר.

3. יי מֶלֶךְ יי מָלָךְ יי יִמְלֹךְ לְעוֹלָם וָעֶד

4. יי עֹז לְעַמּוֹ יִתֵּן יי יְבָרֵךְ אֶת־עַמּוֹ בַשָּׁלוֹם.

5. אַב הָרַחֲמִים הֵיטִיבָה בִרְצוֹנְךָ אֶת־צִיּוֹן.

6. וַיְהִי בִּנְסֹעַ הָאָרֹן וַיֹּאמֶר מֹשֶׁה.

7. קוּמָה יי וְיָפֻצוּ אֹיְבֶיךָ וְיָנֻסוּ מְשַׂנְאֶיךָ מִפָּנֶיךָ.

8. כִּי מִצִּיּוֹן תֵּצֵא תוֹרָה וּדְבַר יי מִירוּשָׁלָיִם.

9. בָּרוּךְ שֶׁנָּתַן תּוֹרָה לְעַמּוֹ יִשְׂרָאֵל בִּקְדֻשָּׁתוֹ.

10. אֶחָד אֱלֹהֵינוּ גָּדוֹל אֲדוֹנֵינוּ קָדוֹשׁ שְׁמוֹ.

11. גַּדְּלוּ לַיי אִתִּי וּנְרוֹמְמָה שְׁמוֹ יַחְדָּו.

12. רוֹמְמוּ יי אֱלֹהֵינוּ וְהִשְׁתַּחֲווּ לַהֲדֹם רַגְלָיו.

נָתַן

עוֹלָם

מֶלֶךְ

אַתָּה

בָּרוּךְ

תּוֹרָה

נָטַע

Your teacher will help you with your translation.

בָּרוּךְ אַתָּה יי אֱלֹהֵינוּ מֶלֶךְ הָעוֹלָם
אֲשֶׁר נָתַן לָנוּ תּוֹרַת אֱמֶת
וְחַיֵּי עוֹלָם נָטַע בְּתוֹכֵנוּ.
בָּרוּךְ אַתָּה יי נוֹתֵן הַתּוֹרָה.

My best guess at the meaning of this prayer is:

_____

_____

_____

_____

Words

truth = אֱמֶת

life = חַי

inside = תּוֹךְ

Word Parts

to/for = לְ/לִ

us, our = ◼נוּ

the = הַ

Commentary

David ha-Levi lived in the 1600s and wrote a commentary on the *Shulḥan Arukh*. He looked at the ending of this בְּרָכָה and noticed that it was in the present tense. He wrote:

The blessing ends נוֹתֵן הַתּוֹרָה, "Who gives the Torah." Why doesn't it say נָתַן הַתּוֹרָה, "Who gave the Torah in a single revelation at Sinai?" The answer is, that every time we study Torah we get new insights. God always gives us the Torah, every day, for we occupy ourselves with it and God helps us find new meanings. (O. Ḥ. 47.5)

Question: Explain this comment in your own words. What did you learn the last time Torah was present tense for you?

The Deaths of the Maharal

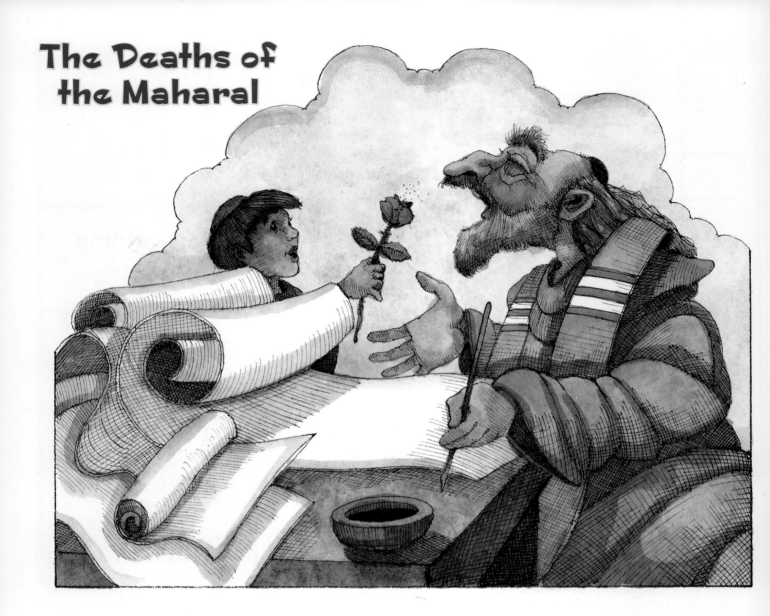

The Torah blessing teaches us that "God has planted within us eternal life." The Talmud makes it clear that Torah is the way that the seed of eternity enters our soul (*Hagigah* 3b). The Maharal, Rabbi Judah Lowe, was a rabbi in Prague in the 1500s. Stories tell that he was the one who made the Golem, an almost-person, out of mud and did many other miracles for the good of the Jewish community. Stories also tell that he knew the secret of eternal life. The Maharal knew that the Angel of Death could not take a person who was studying Torah. As he grew older and older (and he lived eighty-five years) he studied more and more, leaving the Angel of Death no window of opportunity. Still he did die, and two different stories tell how.

The Prague Version

The Maharal could smell the Angel of Death and would always study more intently when he approached. Finally, the Angel of Death made a plan. He hid in a beautiful dark red rose. Once, when the Maharal was studying, his grandson came running up and said, "Grampa, smell this beautiful rose." The Maharal stopped studying, put his book down, and took the flower from his grandson. He breathed it in deeply, and the Angel of Death sadly completed his mission

(J. Funzig in *Die Wundermänner im Judischen Volk*).

47

Just before the High Holy Days the Maharal was studying in the synagogue late into the night. He thought he was alone, then saw a man enter and start to sharpen a big knife. The man was looking at a long list of names. Suddenly the Maharal realized that this man was no man. He was the Angel of Death. The list was the list of those who would live and those who would die in the next year. He grabbed the list out of the Angel's hand and ran home. The bottom corner of the list tore off and stayed with the Angel. The Maharal went through the list and was relieved to find that he had gotten the names of everyone in the community. They should be safe. The Maharal died right after the holidays. He had forgotten to check for his own name (J. Bergmann's *Die Legenden der Juden*).

Questions

1. What lessons about life do these stories of the Maharal's death teach?
2. Where is the "eternal life" in each story?
3. How can knowing these stories help you to point your heart when you say or hear the closing Torah blessing?

Reviewing the Torah Blessings

Some things to know

- Reading the Torah is like eating. We say blessings before and after it.
- Torah gives us eternal life.

Language Learning

Roots: נ ת ן

Words:

 בָּרוּךְ   אַתָּה   מֶלֶךְ   עוֹלָם   תּוֹרָה   נָתַן   נָטַע

 עֲצֹר!

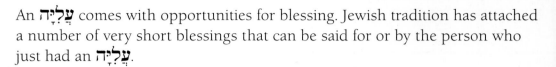

An **עֲלִיָה** comes with opportunities for blessing. Jewish tradition has attached a number of very short blessings that can be said for or by the person who just had an **עֲלִיָה**.

The Bar/Bat Mitzvah בְּרָכָה

In the Midrash we are told that when Jacob and Esau turned thirteen, Isaac said the bar mitzvah **בְּרָכָה**. He said, "**בָּרוּךְ שֶׁפְּטָרַנִי מֵעָנְשׁוֹ שֶׁל זֶה**." "Blessed be the One who has freed me from this child's punishment."

The idea of this blessing is that when children turn thirteen, they become old enough to be responsible for their own actions. In traditional synagogues parents now say this blessing. However, in many synagogues the **שֶׁהֶחֱיָנוּ**, the blessing that celebrates holy moments, is said in addition to or instead of this formula.

Saying גּוֹמֵל

גּוֹמֵל is a prayer that is said after having survived a dangerous situation. It is a special thank you to God for having come through the danger. This is based on a verse in the Psalms that says "Let them thank Adonai for God's mercy and for the wonders done for people" (Psalm 107.8). The Talmud requires a person who survives a serious injury or illness, has gone on a dangerous journey, or has been released from imprisonment to say a prayer (*Brakhot* 54b). In many synagogues a person who needs to say **גּוֹמֵל** is given an **עֲלִיָה** and says the prayer after finishing their closing **בְּרָכָה**.

מִי שֶׁבֵּרַךְ

מִי שֶׁבֵּרַךְ is a chance for the congregation to ask God's blessing on the person(s) who just had an **עֲלִיָה**. Sometimes this is done in a standard way. If you have an **עֲלִיָה**, you get a **מִי שֶׁבֵּרַךְ**. Sometimes, if something special is happening in your life—if you have had a baby, if you are getting married, if there is some other honor—the congregation gives you an **עֲלִיָה** so that you can be given a **מִי שֶׁבֵּרַךְ**. More and more, older traditions that use **מִי שֶׁבֵּרַךְ** as an opportunity to ask God for healing are becoming part of congregational life. Many congregations invite everyone to contribute the names of people in need of healing.

מִי שֶׁבֵּרַךְ is a moment when a congregation celebrates being a community. It is a chance to celebrate and seek strength with each other.

In this unit you will learn:
• About מִי שֶׁבֵּרַךְ
• Roots: עלה

49

מִי שֶׁבֵּרַךְ

FOR A MAN/WOMAN CALLED UP TO THE TORAH

May the One who BLESSED our ancestors (fathers and mothers)	מִי שֶׁבֵּרַךְ אֲבוֹתֵינוּ וְאִמּוֹתֵינוּ	1.
Abraham, Isaac, and Jacob	אַבְרָהָם יִצְחָק וְיַעֲקֹב	2.
Sarah, Rivkah, Rachel, and Leah	שָׂרָה רִבְקָה רָחֵל וְלֵאָה	4.
May God Bless _____ son of _____	הוּא יְבָרֵךְ אֶת ___ בֶּן ___	5.
May God Bless _____ daughter of _____	הוּא יְבָרֵךְ אֶת ___ בַּת ___	
who had an aliyah today to HONOR God	שֶׁעָלָה/שֶׁעָלְתָה הַיּוֹם לִכְבוֹד הַמָּקוֹם	6.
to HONOR the Torah and to HONOR the Shabbat.	לִכְבוֹד הַתּוֹרָה וְלִכְבוֹד הַשַּׁבָּת.	7.
May the Holy One	הַקָּדוֹשׁ בָּרוּךְ הוּא	8.
GUARD him/her	יִשְׁמֹר אוֹתוֹ/אוֹתָהּ	9.
and all his/her family	וְאֶת־כָּל־מִשְׁפַּחְתּוֹ/מִשְׁפַּחְתָּהּ	10.
and send BLESSING and SUCCESS	וְיִשְׁלַח בְּרָכָה וְהַצְלָחָה	11.
on all the WORKS OF his/her HANDS	בְּכָל־מַעֲשֵׂה יָדָיו/יָדֶיהָ	12.
with all of Israel his/her siblings	עִם כָּל־יִשְׂרָאֵל אֶחָיו/אַחֶיהָ	13.
and let us say, "Amen."	וְנֹאמַר אָמֵן.	14.

NOTE: There is no fixed text for מִי שֶׁבֵּרַךְ. Different *siddurim* offer different texts for different situations. It is more an opportunity than a fixed set of words.

The מִי שֶׁבֵּרַךְ is not a magical incantation. It obligates the עוֹלֶה to give צְדָקָה and to pray personally on behalf of the person for whom the prayer is given. It summons us all to recognize our own utter powerlessness in the face of illness (Danny Landes, *My People's Prayer Book*).

Rabbi Yehudah, son of Rabbi Ḥiyya, taught, "Come and see how the works of humans are not like those of the Holy One. When one human gives a drug to another it helps one part of the body but harms another. But when the Holy One gives Torah to Israel, it is a drug of life for the whole body, as it is taught: 'Healing all the flesh'" (Prov. 4.22) (*Eruvin* 54a).

Question: How is the Torah a source of healing?

Can you see the three letters עלה in these words?

עוֹלָה   עֲלִיָּה   יַעֲלוּ

go up to the Torah/Israel = עֲלִיָּה
sacrifice to God = עוֹלָה
they will bring up = יַעֲלוּ

Practice these phrases from the Torah that contain the root עלה.

Gen. 2:6	וְאֵד יַעֲלֶה מִן־הָאָרֶץ וְהִשְׁקָה אֶת־כָּל־פְּנֵי הָאֲדָמָה	.1
Gen. 28:12	וְהִנֵּה מַלְאֲכֵי אֱלֹהִים עֹלִים וְיֹרְדִים בּוֹ	.2
Gen. 37:28	וַיַּעֲלוּ אֶת־יוֹסֵף מִן־הַבּוֹר וַיִּמְכְּרוּ אֶת־יוֹסֵף לַיִּשְׁמְעֵאלִים	.3
Ex. 17:3	וַיֹּאמֶר לָמָּה זֶּה הֶעֱלִיתָנוּ מִמִּצְרַיִם לְהָמִית אֹתִי	.4
Ex. 40:36	וּבְהֵעָלוֹת הֶעָנָן מֵעַל הַמִּשְׁכָּן יִסְעוּ בְּנֵי יִשְׂרָאֵל	.5
Lev. 1:9	וְהִקְטִיר הַכֹּהֵן אֶת־הַכֹּל הַמִּזְבֵּחָה עֹלָה אִשֵּׁה רֵיחַ־נִיחוֹחַ לַי״	.6
Lev. 16:5	יִקַּח שְׁנֵי־שְׂעִירֵי עִזִּים לְחַטָּאת וְאַיִל אֶחָד לְעֹלָה	.7
Num. 20:25	קַח אֶת־אַהֲרֹן וְאֶת־אֶלְעָזָר בְּנוֹ וְהַעַל אֹתָם הֹר הָהָר	.8
Deut. 29:22	לֹא תִזָּרַע וְלֹא תַצְמִחַ וְלֹא־יַעֲלֶה בָהּ כָּל־עֵשֶׂב	.9

 שָׂרָה

 יַעֲקֹב

 יִצְחָק

 אַבְרָהָם

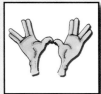 אָב

 בָּרוּךְ

 רִבְקָה

 לֵאָה

 רָחֵל

 עָלָה

מִי שֶׁבֵּרַךְ אֲבוֹתֵינוּ אַבְרָהָם יִצְחָק וְיַעֲקֹב

שָׂרָה רִבְקָה רָחֵל וְלֵאָה

הוּא יְבָרֵךְ אֶת ___ בֶּן/בַּת _____

שֶׁעָלָה/שֶׁעָלְתָה הַיּוֹם

לִכְבוֹד הַמָּקוֹם לִכְבוֹד הַתּוֹרָה וְלִכְבוֹד הַשַּׁבָּת

Your teacher will help you with your translation.

My best guess at the meaning of this prayer is:

May the one who blessed our ancestors, Abraham, Isaac, and Jacob, Sarah, Rivkah, Rachel and Leah. May god bless ___ son/daughter of ___ who had an aliyah today to HONOR god to HONOR The torah and to HONOR the Shabbat

 עֲצֹר!

 יוֹם

 כָּבוֹד

 תּוֹרָה

 שַׁבָּת

Words

who = מִי

son = בֶּן

daughter = בַּת

place/God = מָקוֹם

Word Parts

which, who, that = שֶׁ

52

Reading for Health

1. הוּא יְבָרֵךְ וִירַפֵּא אֶת-הַחוֹלָה

2. וְיִשְׁלַח לוֹ מְהֵרָה רְפוּאָה שְׁלֵמָה לְכָל-אֵבָרָיו

3. וְגִדְיָה בְּתוֹךְ שְׁאָר חוֹלֵי יִשְׂרָאֵל רְפוּאַת הַנֶּפֶשׁ וּרְפוּאַת הַגּוּף

4. יִזְכּוּ הוֹרֶיהָ לְגַדְּלָהּ לְתוֹרָה וּלְחוּפָּה וּלְמַעֲשִׂים טוֹבִים

5. הוּא יְבָרֵךְ אֶת __ בֶּן __ שֶׁהִגִּיעַ לְמִצְווֹת וְעָלָה לַתּוֹרָה

6. וְיִמְצָא חֵן וְשֵׂכֶל טוֹב בְּעֵינֵי אֱלֹהִים וְאָדָם וְנֹאמַר אָמֵן

7. הַקָּדוֹשׁ בָּרוּךְ הוּא יִשְׁמְרֵהוּ וִיחַיֵּהוּ וִיכוֹנֵן אֶת-לִבּוֹ לִהְיוֹת שָׁלֵם

8. הוּא יְבָרֵךְ אֶת-כָּל-הַקְּרוּאִים אֲשֶׁר עָלוּ הַיּוֹם לִכְבוֹד הַמָּקוֹם

9. לַהֲגוֹת בְּתוֹרָתוֹ לָלֶכֶת בִּדְרָכָיו וְלִשְׁמוֹר מִצְווֹתָיו וְתִמְצָא חֵן

10. הוּא יְבָרֵךְ אֶת-הָאִשָּׁה הַיּוֹלֶדֶת וְאֶת-הַיַּלְדָּה הַנּוֹלְדָה לָהּ בְּמַזָּל טוֹב

11. וְיִשְׁלַח בְּרָכָה וְהַצְלָחָה בְּכָל-מַעֲשֵׂה יְדֵיהֶם עִם כָּל-יִשְׂרָאֵל אֲחֵיהֶם

יָד   עָשָׂה   שָׁלַח   בָּרוּךְ   קָדוֹשׁ

יִשְׂרָאֵל

Your teacher will help you with your translation.

הַקָּדוֹשׁ בָּרוּךְ הוּא יְבָרֵךְ אוֹתוֹ/אוֹתָהּ

וְאֶת־כָּל־מִשְׁפַּחְתּוֹ/מִשְׁפַּחְתָּהּ

וְיִשְׁלַח בְּרָכָה וְהַצְלָחָה בְּכָל־מַעֲשֵׂה יָדָיו/יָדֶיהָ

עִם כָּל־יִשְׂרָאֵל אֶחָיו/אֲחֶיהָ וְנֹאמַר אָמֵן

(Words)

him = אוֹתוֹ

her = אוֹתָהּ

all = כֹּל

family = מִשְׁפָּחָה

success = הַצְלָחָה

brother = אַח

said = אָמַר

My best guess at the meaning of this prayer is:

_____

_____

_____

_____

Healing

The מִי שֶׁבֵּרַךְ can also be a time for prayers of healing. The Midrash teaches the following:

Said the Holy One, "There is no sickness for which a cure does not exist—somewhere— there is a therapy or medicine for every medical problem. If you want to be well, study Torah, for it is a therapy for the whole body" (*Midrash Tanḥuma, Yitro,* 8).

Questions

1. In what ways is this a true statement?
2. In what ways are there problems with this statement?
3. How can prayer and study help to make a person well?

54

God's Partner

Abraham Joshua Heschel was the rabbi of Apt in the 1800s. He once heard that in a village near his city there was a shopkeeper who was doing miracles. If a person was sick and he asked God's blessing for him or her, that person got better. When he prayed for a person to succeed in business, that person's business improved. No one could figure out why the shopkeeper's prayers seemed to be so effective—there was nothing particularly unusual about him.

Finally, after hearing more and more stories about the miracle-working shopkeeper, Rabbi Abraham went and directly asked him, "Why does God listen to your prayers?" The shopkeeper said, "I don't really know why. Perhaps it is because I trust God.

"Whenever I am distressed, whenever things go wrong, I give away much of what I have to help others. The helping others often helps me. Once I was feeding a poor man when a government official showed up and demanded that I go with him. Because feeding the poor is a mitzvah that comes from God, I told the official I could not go until I finished a task for a higher authority. He said 'Okay' and never came back.

"Once I lost almost everything I owned when business turned bad. My wife quoted an old Jewish saying, 'Change your location and change your luck.' She told me to go to another town and find a partner to go into business with me. I left and started to look for a partner, but then I asked myself, 'Why should I trust a human partner when I can ask God to be my partner? I can trust no human partner the way I trust God.' I asked God to be my partner. I went home, managed to borrow some money, and got back into business. Since that day I have kept two cash boxes in my business. I put half the money in one box for me and half the money in the other box for God. God's money I use for צְדָקָה."

When Rabbi Abraham heard this he said, "I understand when one partner makes a commitment, Jewish law says that the other partner must help to fulfill it. When the shop owner makes a commitment, God must help with it..." (taken from Rabbi Abraham J. Twersky, *Prayerfully Yours*).

Questions

1. Was it a good move or a foolish move for this store owner to take God as his partner?
2. Do you believe that his good deeds helped his prayers to be effective?
3. We frequently use the term "God's partner" to talk about the things that we should do to help God improve the world. Partnerships work two ways. What are the things we should trust God to do for us?
4. How can knowing this story help you point your heart when you hear, receive, or ask for a "מִי שֶׁבֵּרַךְ"?

Reviewing מִי שֶׁבֵּרַךְ

Some things to know

Various blessings are attached to an עֲלִיָּה:

- The bar/bat mitzvah בְּרָכָה—a statement of independence.
- גּוֹמֵל—a prayer after escaping a danger
- מִי שֶׁבֵּרַךְ—a request for blessing.

Language Learning

Root: עלה   Words:

בָּרוּךְ   יוֹם   כָּבוֹד   תּוֹרָה   שַׁבָּת   קָדוֹשׁ

שָׁלַח   עָשָׂה   יָד   יִשְׂרָאֵל

עֲצֹר!

וְזֹאת הַתּוֹרָה

הַגְבָּהָה is a ceremony that happens during the Torah reading. Sefardic Jews do הַגְבָּהָה before the reading from the Torah. Ashkenazic Jews do הַגְבָּהָה after the reading from the Torah. During הַגְבָּהָה the Torah scroll is held up and the columns that were or are to be read are shown to the congregation.

הַגְבָּהָה is the acting out of a story we read about in the book of Nehemiah. When the Jews came home from the Babylonian Exile they had trouble getting organized and unified. Ezra the Scribe came with a סֵפֶר תּוֹרָה and gathered the people at the Water Gate. The Torah was read from beginning to end, and reading the Torah became a new beginning for the Jewish people. As part of the ceremony, Ezra had the text of the Torah shown to the people. It brought the words of the Torah off the stage and into direct contact with each of the people who were gathered to hear the reading.

Today, when we lift the Torah as part of the הַגְבָּהָה ceremony, it is a tradition to hold up one of the צִיצִיּוֹת (fringes) on our טַלִית that we then bring to our lips. It is as if we are kissing the very words we have read (or are to read). We also sing a prayer assembled out of a number of biblical verses. These phrases that begin "וְזֹאת הַתּוֹרָה" connect the words of the Torah to God.

In this unit you will learn:
- About הַגְבָּהָה
- זֹאת הַתּוֹרָה

וְזֹאת הַתּוֹרָה

This is the TORAH	1. וְזֹאת הַתּוֹרָה
that MOSES gave	2. אֲשֶׁר שָׂם מֹשֶׁה
to The-FAMILIES-of-ISRAEL (Deut. 4.44)	3. לִפְנֵי בְּנֵי יִשְׂרָאֵל
from the MOUTH of ADONAI	4. עַל פִּי יי
through the HAND of MOSES (Num. 9.23).	5. בְּיַד מֹשֶׁה.

Choreography: הַגְבָּהָה

Before or after the last Torah reading the Torah is lifted in the air. This ritual is called הַגְבָּהָה, lifting. The person with this honor comes to the בִּימָה and lifts the Torah in the air with at least three columns of the text showing. That person turns around so that the whole congregation can see the text. During this ceremony we sing וְזֹאת הַתּוֹרָה. It is a tradition for congregants to wrap one of the fringes of their טַלִית around their little finger and hold it up in the air toward the open scroll. When the scroll is brought down, people bring that צִיצִית (fringe) to their lips. It is as if they are taking the words off the scroll and bringing them to their mouths.

פֶּה

עַל

יִשְׂרָאֵל

בָּנִים

מֹשֶׁה

תוֹרָה

יָד

(Words)

this = זֹאת

that = אֲשֶׁר

put = שָׂם

before = לִפְנֵי

(Word Parts)

and = וְ

Your teacher will help you with your translation.

וְזֹאת הַתּוֹרָה אֲשֶׁר שָׂם מֹשֶׁה לִפְנֵי בְּנֵי יִשְׂרָאֵל עַל פִּי יי בְּיַד מֹשֶׁה.

My best guess at the meaning of this prayer is:

_____

_____

_____

How I Learned to Study Torah

There was a ten-year-old boy who refused to study Torah. His parents tried all the usual parent things, yelling, punishing, begging and crying. None of these worked. When the greatest Hasidic rebbe of their generation, Aaron of Karlin, visited their little shtetl, they brought the problem to him. The rebbe looked at the little boy, who stood defiantly. His gaze was down; his arms were folded. The rebbe told the parents, "Leave him here with me for two hours. I'll give him a talking-to that he'll never forget!"

As soon as the parents had left, the rebbe went up to the little boy and slowly, tenderly, put his arms around him. The boy was stiff at first but then slowly allowed himself to be hugged. He relaxed and was finally squeezed against the breast of the great man. He stood there, hearing the rebbe's heartbeat. Their breath flowed in and out together.

On the way home, the parents looked at their little boy, wondering, was there any change? They stopped at the butcher's. The

59

butcher slapped a piece of meat on the counter. The boy asked, "That butcher is angry. What happened to him to make him feel that way?"

From then on, the boy was somehow more in touch with people, attuned to their feelings, interested in their stories. That week when he heard others discussing the Torah he suddenly realized that the Torah was the stories of people! He became fascinated with them. What made the people act that way?

Immediately he began to read the stories for himself. Within a year his teachers saw him as their most talented student. Once two neighbors were arguing over the purchase of a calf. The boy went up to them and said, "There's a way for both of you to get what you want." He showed them a workable compromise. Before long adult villagers were bringing their quarrels to the boy, and he would point out to them the solutions that had been there in their hearts.

Years later, when he was known as the greatest rebbe of his generation, his disciples would sit around him and ask: "How did you get your deep insight into the Torah?" The boy, now the rebbe, answered: "I learned everything when the rabbi, Aaron of Karlin, hugged me."

(Retold from a telling by Doug Lipman from *Chosen Tales*, edited by Peninnah Schram)

Questions
1. What change in the boy helped him to become a great Torah student?
2. What does this story teach us about the nature of the Torah?
3. How can knowing this story help you point your heart when you sing וְזֹאת הַתּוֹרָה?

Reviewing וְזֹאת הַתּוֹרָה

Some things to know

- הַגְבָּהָה is a ceremony where, like Ezra, we show the text of the Torah to the congregation.
- וְזֹאת הַתּוֹרָה is the prayer said during this ceremony.

Language Learning

Words:

| תּוֹרָה | מֹשֶׁה | בָּנִים | יִשְׂרָאֵל | עַל | פֶּה | יָד |

עֲצֹר!

Haftarah Blessings

הַפְטָרָה is not "half-Torah." It comes from a Hebrew root that means "completion." The הַפְטָרָה is a selection from the Prophets that is read after the Torah portion on Shabbat and holidays as the "completion" of the Torah reading.

The origins of the הַפְטָרָה readings are not clear. The oldest story about the הַפְטָרָה is this. Before the story of *Hanukkah* happened, before the Jews fought back, Antiochus IV banned many Jewish practices. Among the new rules he created was "No more reading Torah." Jews were good at getting around such orders. Antiochus banned Torah readings, not readings from the Prophets. So they created the הַפְטָרָה. They picked passages from the Prophets that reminded them of the Torah readings. They read these passages as a replacement for the Torah portion of the week. Later, when they could again read Torah, these passages were kept and added to the weekly readings (*Sefer Abudarham*).

The reading of the הַפְטָרָה is very much like the reading of the Torah. There are blessings that are said before and after it. One blessing is said before the reading of the הַפְטָרָה. Traditionally four blessings are said after the הַפְטָרָה reading, though the Reform movement only says one of them.

The person who reads the הַפְטָרָה is called the מַפְטִיר. Traditionally, the person who is the מַפְטִיר also has the last עֲלִיָּה of the Torah reading. The הַפְטָרָה is usually read out of a book (although some congregations have scrolls) and has its own trope (melodies used for chanting). In addition to one הַפְטָרָה portion for every Torah portion, there are special הַפְטָרָה readings for Jewish holidays and other special שַׁבָּתוֹת.

In this unit you will learn:
• About the הַפְטָרָה.
• The root בחר

61

Opening Haftarah Blessing

Blessed be You, ADONAI,	בָּרוּךְ אַתָּה יי	.1
Ruler of the cosmos	אֱלֹהֵינוּ מֶלֶךְ הָעוֹלָם	.2
Who CHOSE good PROPHETS	אֲשֶׁר בָּחַר בִּנְבִיאִים טוֹבִים	.3
and wanted the words	וְרָצָה בְדִבְרֵיהֶם	.4
the TRUE words they spoke.	הַנֶּאֱמָרִים בֶּאֱמֶת.	.5
Blessed be You, ADONAI,	בָּרוּךְ אַתָּה יי	.6
Who CHOOSE the TORAH,	הַבּוֹחֵר בַּתּוֹרָה	.7
and MOSES God's servant	וּבְמֹשֶׁה עַבְדּוֹ	.8
and ISRAEL God's people	וּבְיִשְׂרָאֵל עַמּוֹ	.9
and the PROPHETS of TRUTH and JUSTICE.	וּבִנְבִיאֵי הָאֱמֶת וָצֶדֶק.	.10

Commentary

What is a prophet? The prophets were people who were called to spread among the Jewish people the understanding of the Law of God as set down in the Torah. The prophets were to serve as God's agents, warning and cautioning the people. It was their job to interpret the Word of God and to offer consolation, to teach the true meaning of the joy that comes from obeying the law and the misfortune that comes from disobedience (Samson Raphael Hirsch, *The Hirsch Siddur*).

Question: According to Rabbi Hirsch, what is a prophet?

Can you see the three letters בחר in these words?

בָּחַר הַבּוֹחֵר בְּחַרְתָּנוּ

בָּחַר = chose

הַבּוֹחֵר = the One Who chooses

בְּחַרְתָּנוּ = You have chosen us

Practice these phrases and circle all the words that contain the root בחר.

1. בָּרוּךְ אַתָּה יי הַבּוֹחֵר בְּעַמּוֹ יִשְׂרָאֵל בְּאַהֲבָה

2. זֶרַע יִשְׂרָאֵל עַבְדּוֹ בְּנֵי יַעֲקֹב בְּחִירָיו

3. אֲשֶׁר בָּחַר בָּנוּ מִכָּל־הָעַמִּים וְנָתַן לָנוּ אֶת־תּוֹרָתוֹ

4. אַתָּה בְחַרְתָּנוּ מִכָּל־הָעַמִּים אָהַבְתָּ אוֹתָנוּ וְרָצִיתָ בָּנוּ

5. בָּרוּךְ אַתָּה יי הַבּוֹחֵר בַּתּוֹרָה וּבְמֹשֶׁה עַבְדּוֹ וּבְיִשְׂרָאֵל עַמּוֹ

6. כִּי יַעֲקֹב בָּחַר לוֹ יָהּ יִשְׂרָאֵל לִסְגֻלָּתוֹ כִּי לֹא יִטֹּשׁ יי עַמּוֹ

7. כִּי אֵל פּוֹעֵל יְשׁוּעוֹת אַתָּה וּבָנוּ בָחַרְתָּ מִכָּל־עָם וְלָשׁוֹן

8. אֲדוֹן הַנִּפְלָאוֹת הַבּוֹחֵר בְּשִׁירֵי זִמְרָה מֶלֶךְ אֵל חֵי הָעוֹלָמִים

9. הַבּוֹחֵר בַּתּוֹרָה וּבְמֹשֶׁה עַבְדּוֹ וּבְיִשְׂרָאֵל עַמּוֹ וּבִנְבִיאֵי הָאֱמֶת וָצֶדֶק

נָבִיא

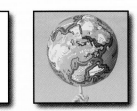

בָּחַר

עוֹלָם

מֶלֶךְ

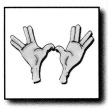

אַתָּה

בָּרוּךְ

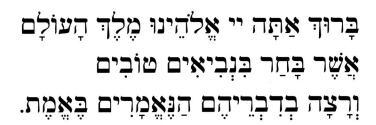

Your teacher will help you with your translation.

טוֹב

דִּבֶּר

(Words)

that = אֲשֶׁר

want = רָצָה

said = אָמַר

truth = אֱמֶת

בָּרוּךְ אַתָּה יי אֱלֹהֵינוּ מֶלֶךְ הָעוֹלָם
אֲשֶׁר בָּחַר בִּנְבִיאִים טוֹבִים
וְרָצָה בְדִבְרֵיהֶם הַנֶּאֱמָרִים בֶּאֱמֶת.

My best guess at the meaning of this prayer is:

_____

_____

_____

Commentary

What do the words אֲשֶׁר בָּחַר בִּנְבִיאִים טוֹבִים teach?

God chose as prophets only טוֹבִים (good people). A person who is called a true prophet must be חָכָם (wise), גִּבּוֹר (a hero), and עָשִׁיר (rich). That means a prophet must have knowledge and wisdom absorbed from the Torah. A prophet must be strong and healthy of both body and spirit so that nothing can lead him or her astray. And a prophet must be rich, meaning that a prophet is completely satisfied with what he or she has. Finally, a true prophet must be really טוֹב (good) and a friend to all people. Without good there can be neither peace nor salvation. The רוּחַ הַקֹּדֶשׁ (the Holy Spirit) that comes from God is also called the רוּחַ הַטּוֹב (the good spirit) (Samson Raphael Hirsch, *The Hirsch Siddur*).

Question: According to Rabbi Hirsch, what kind of person can be a prophet? What do we have to do to become like a prophet?

The Prophets (A Job Description)

In his book *The Prophets*, Abraham Joshua Heschel (whose grandfather was the rabbi of Apt) says "Prophets were some of the most disturbing people who have ever lived, people whose inspiration brought the Bible into being—people whose image is a refuge in distress and whose voice and vision sustain our faith. The significance of Israel's prophets lies not only in what they said, but also what they were."

While many people use prophet to mean "one who predicts the future"—a kind of fortuneteller—that is not the Jewish understanding. Many people try to predict the future. Some succeed and some fail. For Jews, prophets are people who help us to understand the way that God wants us to build the future and who warn us about futures that should not come to be.

Heschel set up a job description for prophets:

- **Prophets are sensitive to evil**. They notice people being hurt when others can walk by and not notice.

- **Prophets can glow and prophets can explode**. They can inspire others to rethink their lives. They can rage with anger against that which is wrong.

- **Prophets seek the highest good.** They will settle for nothing less.

- **Prophets smash idols.** They literally smash idols—and they shatter many things that give us comfort but that are less than God wants from us.

- **Prophets live simply but have great compassion.** They want little for themselves, but they care greatly about others.

- **The prophets often say, "Few are guilty, but all are responsible."** For them, "Not my fault" doesn't work.

- **Prophets are a blast for Heaven.** They are weapons for truth and justice—for making sure that God is heard.

- **Prophets are often lonely and unhappy.** They are often not liked. They are often unpleasant people because they do not give in or compromise.

- **Prophets test people, they challenge people, they are witnesses for things people would like to forget, and most of all they are messengers for God.** Prophets have the job of changing the world or making sure that we always do what is right rather than what is easy, that we always do what is just even if it is difficult or uncomfortable.

Questions

1. Why do you think that prophets do what they do?
2. Would you like to be a prophet?
3. Are there times when you act like a prophet? Are there times when you need to act like a prophet?
4. Who in our world today is like a biblical prophet?

65

Prophetic Writing in the Liturgy

Practice these phrases from the Prophets.

1. לֹא יִשָּׂא גוֹי אֶל גוֹי חֶרֶב וְלֹא יִלְמְדוּ עוֹד מִלְחָמָה

Isaiah 2.4

2. קָדוֹשׁ קָדוֹשׁ קָדוֹשׁ יי צְבָאוֹת מְלֹא־כָל הָאָרֶץ כְּבוֹדוֹ

Isaiah 6.3

3. בָּרוּךְ כְּבוֹד יי מִמְּקוֹמוֹ

Ezekiel 3.12

4. בַּיּוֹם הַהוּא יִהְיֶה יי אֶחָד וּשְׁמוֹ אֶחָד

Zechariah 14.9

5. הִנֵּה אֵל יְשׁוּעָתִי אֶבְטַח וְלֹא אֶפְחָד

Isaiah 12.2

6. עֻצוּ עֵצָה וְתֻפָר דַּבְּרוּ דָבָר וְלֹא יָקוּם כִּי עִמָּנוּ אֵל

Isaiah 8.10

7. מַה־נָּאווּ עַל־הֶהָרִים רַגְלֵי מְבַשֵּׂר מַשְׁמִיעַ שָׁלוֹם מְבַשֵּׂר טוֹב

Isaiah 52:7

8. הֲבֵן יַקִּיר לִי אֶפְרַיִם אִם יֶלֶד שַׁעֲשׁוּעִים כִּי־מִדֵּי דַבְּרִי בּוֹ

Jeremiah 31.20

9. וְזָכַרְתִּי אֲנִי אֶת־בְּרִיתִי אוֹתָךְ מִימֵי נְעוּרָיִךְ

Ezekiel 16.60

10. יי חָפֵץ לְמַעַן צִדְקוֹ יַגְדִּיל תּוֹרָה וְיַאְדִּיר

Isaiah 42.21

11. וַיִּגְבַּה יי צְבָאוֹת בַּמִּשְׁפָּט וְהָאֵל הַקָּדוֹשׁ נִקְדָּשׁ בִּצְדָקָה

Isaiah 5:16

עֶבֶד

מֹשֶׁה

תּוֹרָה

בָּחַר

אַתָּה

בָּרוּךְ

יִשְׂרָאֵל

נָבִיא

צְדָקָה

Your teacher will help you with your translation.

בָּרוּךְ אַתָּה יי הַבּוֹחֵר בַּתּוֹרָה וּבְמֹשֶׁה עַבְדּוֹ
וּבְיִשְׂרָאֵל עַמּוֹ וּבִנְבִיאֵי הָאֱמֶת וָצֶדֶק

My best guess at the meaning of this prayer is:

_____

_____

_____

(Words)

nation = עַם■

(Word Parts)

in/with = בְּ

the = הַ

His = ■וֹ

and = וְ/וּ

Commentary

Why does בִּרְכַּת הַהַפְטָרָה mention both Moses and the prophets?

God made the words of the prophets equal to the Torah. That is why there are five בְּרָכוֹת that surround the הַפְטָרָה (Abudarham).

Questions

1. How do five בְּרָכוֹת teach that the הַפְטָרָה is equal to the Torah?

2. What does it mean that the prophets are equal to the Torah?

The Real Jew

Rabbi Mendele Sokolover had a mission. He was looking for "a real Jew." He went on a search for a Jew who fully lived a life of Torah. The rabbi found many good Jews, but he found the person he was looking for in Moshe, the water carrier. A water carrier was a person who was paid a few pennies to draw water out of the well and then carry buckets of water to the houses of the rich. Water carrier was a low-level job from the days before indoor plumbing.

Moshe lived in Sokolov, and when he was not carrying water he could usually be found with a book of Psalms in his hand. When Mendele became the rabbi of Sokolov he tried to talk to Moshe, but the man said little. One night the rabbi was walking through the streets of the town and found a party of water carriers, shoemakers, and tailors. There he learned the story of "a true Jew."

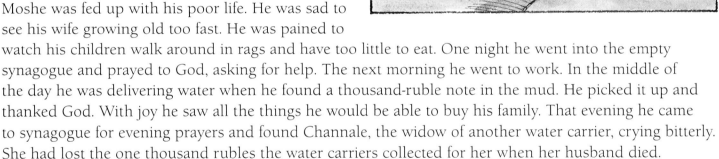

Moshe was fed up with his poor life. He was sad to see his wife growing old too fast. He was pained to watch his children walk around in rags and have too little to eat. One night he went into the empty synagogue and prayed to God, asking for help. The next morning he went to work. In the middle of the day he was delivering water when he found a thousand-ruble note in the mud. He picked it up and thanked God. With joy he saw all the things he would be able to buy his family. That evening he came to synagogue for evening prayers and found Channale, the widow of another water carrier, crying bitterly. She had lost the one thousand rubles the water carriers collected for her when her husband died.

Moshe did not go into the *shul* to pray. He began screaming at God. "Why did You have to give me Channale's rubles? What kind of God are You? I don't want to have anything to do with You anymore." Then Moshe did what he knew he had to do. He found Channale and returned the money. At that moment his whole life changed. He said, "I knew that my life would never be different. I knew that my children would always wear used clothing. I knew that there would never be enough food on our table. But I knew how good it felt to be a Jew and to live the Torah." His friends made a party in his honor, and the rabbi joined them.

(From a story told by by Annette Labovitz & Eugene Labovitz in *Time for My Soul, A Treasury of Jewish Stories for Our Holy Days*)

Questions

1. The opening הַפְטָרָה blessing says "Who CHOOSES the TORAH, and MOSES God's servant and ISRAEL God's people and the PROPHETS of TRUTH and JUSTICE." Where is the "prophet of truth and justice" in this story?
2. What made Moshe "a true Jew"? How would you define "a true Jew"?
3. How can knowing this story help you point your heart when you read or hear the הַפְטָרָה blessings?

הַפְטָרָה after the בְּרָכוֹת

Reading the Torah is a lot like eating. Reading the הַפְטָרָה is a lot like reading the Torah. We say a blessing before and after eating, and we do the same with Torah (*Brakhot* 21a). Based on the Torah pattern, we say blessings before and after the הַפְטָרָה (and before and after the Purim Megillah, too).

Question: Why should the Torah and הַפְטָרָה follow the same blessing pattern as eating?

Blessing One (Before the הַפְטָרָה): This בְּרָכָה thanks God for the prophets and states that their words are true. Here we state that the truth that came through Moses into the Torah is continued in the teaching of the prophets.

Blessing Two (After the הַפְטָרָה): The central theme of this בְּרָכָה is the statement that God is "The-One-Whose-every-WORD-is-DEPENDABLE." This blessing is the follow-up of the "God speaks the truth" theme of the opening בְּרָכָה. The next three בְּרָכוֹת will list some of the promises made through the prophets on which we can depend.

Blessing Three: We can "trust" that Jerusalem (and the Temple) will be rebuilt. This does not only mean that the State of Israel will be reborn (the way it was) but that "the exile of the Jewish people" will end.

Blessing Four: Next comes the arrival of the Messiah (or the messianic age). This is the next step in the redemption.

Blessing Five: The last blessing is about שַׁבָּת. It is the wrapup. We read the הַפְטָרָה on שַׁבָּת. שַׁבָּת is like an early taste of עוֹלָם הַבָּא (the world to come). Through the celebration of שַׁבָּת, through the words of the prophets read on שַׁבָּת, we move toward a Messianic future.

The Reform, Conservative, and Reconstructionist movements have all made changes in these blessings.

Blessing after the Haftarah

2

Blessed be You, ADONAI,	בָּרוּךְ אַתָּה יי 1.
our God Ruler-of-the-Cosmos	אֱלֹהֵינוּ מֶלֶךְ הָעוֹלָם 2.
ROCK of all reality	צוּר כָּל־הָעוֹלָמִים 4.
JUST in every generation	צַדִּיק בְּכָל־הַדּוֹרוֹת 5.
The GOD, The DEPENDABLE-One, The One Who SAYS and DOES	הָאֵל הַנֶּאֱמָן הָאוֹמֵר וְעוֹשֶׂה 6.
Who SPEAKS and MAKES REAL—	הַמְדַבֵּר וּמְקַיֵּם 7.
Whose every WORD is TRUE and JUST.	שֶׁכָּל־דְּבָרָיו אֱמֶת וָצֶדֶק. 8.
You are DEPENDABLE—ADONAI our God.	נֶאֱמָן אַתָּה הוּא יי אֱלֹהֵינוּ 9.
And Your WORDS are DEPENDABLE	וְנֶאֱמָנִים דְּבָרֶיךָ 10.
and not one of Your words	וְדָבָר אֶחָד מִדְּבָרֶיךָ 11.
will return empty	אָחוֹר לֹא יָשׁוּב רֵיקָם 12.
because YOU are GOD, RULER and DEPENDABLE-One	כִּי אֵל מֶלֶךְ נֶאֱמָן 13.
and You are the Merciful One.	וְרַחֲמָן אַתָּה. 14.
Blessed be You, ADONAI, the GOD	בָּרוּךְ אַתָּה יי הָאֵל 15.
The One-Whose-every-WORD-is-DEPENDABLE.	הַנֶּאֱמָן בְּכָל־דְּבָרָיו. 16.

3

Have MERCY on ZION	רַחֵם עַל צִיּוֹן 17.
for it is the HOUSE of our LIVES	כִּי הִיא בֵּית חַיֵּינוּ. 18.
the humbled SOULS SAVE	וְלַעֲלוּבַת נֶפֶשׁ תּוֹשִׁיעַ 19.
quickly in our lifetime.	בִּמְהֵרָה בְיָמֵינוּ. 19.
Blessed be You, ADONAI	בָּרוּךְ אַתָּה יי 20.
Who makes ZION REJOICE with her CHILDREN.	מְשַׂמֵּחַ צִיּוֹן בְּבָנֶיהָ. 21.

4

Make us REJOICE	שַׂמְּחֵנוּ 22.
ADONAI, Our God	יי אֱלֹהֵינוּ 23.

70

in ELIJAH the PROPHET, Your SERVANT	בְּאֵלִיָּהוּ הַנָּבִיא עַבְדֶּךָ 24.
and the RULE of the HOUSE OF DAVID Your MESSIAH.	וּבְמַלְכוּת בֵּית דָּוִד מְשִׁיחֶךָ. 25.
Bring him quickly	בִּמְהֵרָה יָבֹא 26.
that our HEARTS can celebrate;	וְיָגֵל לִבֵּנוּ 27.
over his throne	עַל כִּסְאוֹ 28.
Let no stranger sit	לֹא יֵשֵׁב זָר 29.
and let no one inherit his honor	וְלֹא יִנְחֲלוּ עוֹד אֲחֵרִים אֶת־כְּבוֹדוֹ 30.
BECAUSE in Your HOLY NAME	כִּי בְשֵׁם קָדְשְׁךָ 31.
You SWORE that his candle would not go out	נִשְׁבַּעְתָּ לּוֹ שֶׁלֹּא יִכְבֶּה נֵרוֹ 32.
FOREVER and ALWAYS	לְעוֹלָם וָעֶד. 33.
BLESSED are You, ADONAI, SHIELD of DAVID.	בָּרוּךְ אַתָּה יי מָגֵן דָּוִד. 34.
For the TORAH, and for WORSHIP,	עַל הַתּוֹרָה וְעַל הָעֲבוֹדָה 35.
and for the PROPHETS,	וְעַל הַנְּבִיאִים 36.
and for this SHABBAT DAY—	וְעַל יוֹם הַשַּׁבָּת הַזֶּה 37.
that You gave us, ADONAI, our God—	שֶׁנָּתַתָּ לָּנוּ יי אֱלֹהֵינוּ 38.
for HOLINESS and for REST	לִקְדֻשָּׁה וְלִמְנוּחָה 39.
for HONOR and for BEAUTY.	לְכָבוֹד וּלְתִפְאָרֶת. 40.
For all of these, ADONAI, our God,	עַל הַכֹּל יי אֱלֹהֵינוּ 41.
we give THANKS to You	אֲנַחְנוּ מוֹדִים לָךְ 42.
And BLESS You—	וּמְבָרְכִים אוֹתָךְ. 43.
May Your NAME be BLESSED	יִתְבָּרַךְ שִׁמְךָ 44.
in the mouth of all life—always	בְּפִי כָּל־חַי תָּמִיד 45.
FOREVER and BEYOND.	לְעוֹלָם וָעֶד. 46.
BLESSED are You ADONAI	בָּרוּךְ אַתָּה יי 47.
THE One-Who-Makes-SHABBAT HOLY.	מְקַדֵּשׁ הַשַּׁבָּת. 48.

5

Can you see the three letters אמן in these words?

נֶאֱמָן   אֱמוּנָה   אָמֵן

Hebrew builds words out of three-letter roots.

So be it! = אָמֵן

faith = אֱמוּנָה

faithful = נֶאֱמָן

Practice these phrases and circle all the words that contain the root אמן.

2. הָאֵל הַנֶּאֱמָן הָאוֹמֵר וְעוֹשֶׂה   1. וּבִזְמַן קָרִיב וְאִמְרוּ אָמֵן

4. יי אֱלֹהֵינוּ וְנֶאֱמָנִים דְּבָרֶיךָ   3. וּמְקַיֵּם אֱמוּנָתוֹ לִישֵׁנֵי עָפָר

Can you see the root אמר in these words?

וְאִמְרוּ   נֶאֱמַר   אוֹמֵר

say = אוֹמֵר

it was said = נֶאֱמַר

and let us say = וְאִמְרוּ

Practice these phrases and circle all the words that contain the root אמר.

6. הָאֵל הַנֶּאֱמָן הָאוֹמֵר וְעוֹשֶׂה   5. וְנֹאמַר לְפָנָיו שִׁיר חָדָשׁ

8. יַחַד כֻּלָּם הוֹדוּ וְהִמְלִיכוּ וְאָמְרוּ   7. וַיֹּאמֶר יי אֶל-מֹשֶׁה לֵּאמֹר

9. אֲשֶׁר בָּחַר בִּנְבִיאִים טוֹבִים וְרָצָה בְּדִבְרֵיהֶם הַנֶּאֱמָרִים בֶּאֱמֶת

72

צְדָקָה

צוּר

עוֹלָם

מֶלֶךְ

אַתָּה

בָּרוּךְ

אָמֵן

אָמַר

עָשָׂה

Your teacher will help you with your translation.

בָּרוּךְ אַתָּה יי אֱלֹהֵינוּ מֶלֶךְ הָעוֹלָם
צוּר כָּל-הָעוֹלָמִים צַדִּיק בְּכָל-הַדּוֹרוֹת
הָאֵל הַנֶּאֱמָן הָאוֹמֵר וְעוֹשֶׂה הַמְדַבֵּר וּמְקַיֵּם
שֶׁכָּל-דְּבָרָיו אֱמֶת וָצֶדֶק.

My best guess at the meaning of this prayer is:

_____

_____

_____

דִּבֵּר

Words

generation = דּוֹר

fulfill = מְקַיֵּם

truth = אֱמֶת

Word Parts

the = הַ

and = וְ/וּ/וָ

in/with = בְּ

Commentary

What does צוּר כָּל-הָעוֹלָמִים mean?

God is the rock of all times Who champions the cause of the right in every era of history (Samson Raphael Hirsch, *The Hirsch Siddur*).

God is the rock of all worlds, the One who created everything physical (Philip Birnbaum, *The Birnbaum Siddur*).

God is the Being Who is beyond time. God's existence outlives all times (Wolf Yawetz).

עֲצֹר!

Questions

1. Which answer do you like best?
2. What is your understanding of this phrase?

קָדוֹשׁ   נָתַן   שַׁבָּת   נָבִיא   תּוֹרָה   עַל

כָּבוֹד

(Words)

worship = עֲבוֹדָה

to us = לָנוּ

rest = מְנוּחָה

glory = תִּפְאֶרֶת

(Word Parts)

and = וְ/וּ

that = שֶׁ

to/for = לְ

Your teacher will help you with your translation.

עַל הַתּוֹרָה וְעַל הָעֲבוֹדָה וְעַל הַנְּבִיאִים
וְעַל יוֹם הַשַּׁבָּת הַזֶּה שֶׁנָּתַתָּ לָנוּ יי אֱלֹהֵינוּ
לִקְדֻשָּׁה וְלִמְנוּחָה לְכָבוֹד וּלְתִפְאָרֶת...
בָּרוּךְ אַתָּה יי מְקַדֵּשׁ הַשַּׁבָּת.

My best guess at the meaning of this prayer is:

_____

_____

_____

_____

Commentary

The ending of the blessing thanks God for four things: תּוֹרָה, עֲבוֹדָה (the worship service), נְבִיאִים (הַפְטָרָה), and יוֹם הַשַּׁבָּת. As we read the words of the Torah on Shabbat we become aware of the growing holiness that can come from living the words of the Torah. All four of these are gifts that God has given us.

(Samson Raphael Hirsch)

Question:

How do these four things go together?

74

The Clothes That Went to a Wedding

Elijah was the prophet who did not die. He flew up to heaven, alive, in a flaming chariot. Legend teaches that he will come back again, helping to bring the messiah. Legend also teaches that from time to time Elijah comes and visits people, teaching interesting lessons.

Once, dressed like a beggar, Elijah came to join in a wedding. His clothing was torn and dirty. His hair was oily and matted. They threw him out. They thought he was trying to crash the wedding just to eat the free food.

An hour later he returned. This time he was dressed in an expensive suit. He was leaning on a fine cane with a golden handle. On his head was a very elegant sable hat. When he entered the room the guests all stood out of respect for this distinguished visitor. The bride and groom came up to him and asked him to join their table. He nodded and sat near them.

The first course was a piece of gefilte fish. The old man picked up his fish and put it in one of his pockets. He added a scoop of horseradish on top of it. When the soup was served, he poured it into another pocket. This time he asked for the salt and sprinkled a little of it into the soup pocket, saying, "It needed just a little."

Each time a course was served, this stranger shoved it into one of his pockets. The string beans wound up sticking out of his vest.

Finally, the stranger stood, took his glass of wine, said, "A toast to the bride and groom," and then spilled the wine over his sleeve. When he finished, there was complete silence in the room. Many people sat with their mouths open. Elijah let the silence hang while he looked around the

75

room. Then he said, "When I first came here dressed as a beggar, you threw me out. When I returned dressed in expensive clothing you welcomed me and showed me respect. It is obvious that you were respecting my clothes, not me. So when you asked me to join in your feast, I let the clothes eat. They were your real guests." Elijah laughed and then disappeared. Left on the chair was his gold-handled cane.

(classic folktale)

Questions

1. How is Elijah acting as a prophet in this story? What is the "truth" he is teaching?
2. How could this truth help to bring a messianic era?
3. How can knowing this story help you to point your heart when you say or hear the בְּרָכוֹת after reading the הַפְטָרָה?

Reviewing the הַפְטָרָה Blessings

Some things to know

- הַפְטָרָה is the completion of the Torah service. These readings match with the Torah readings.
- The five בְּרָכוֹת that surround the הַפְטָרָה match the five books of the תּוֹרָה.
- The prophets were agents of God who deepened the Torah's message.

Language Learning

Roots:  ,

עֲצֹר!

Words:

בָּרוּךְ   אַתָּה   מֶלֶךְ   עוֹלָם   נָבִיא   טוֹב   דִּבֶּר   מֹשֶׁה

עֶבֶד   יִשְׂרָאֵל   צְדָקָה   עַל   תּוֹרָה   שַׁבָּת   כָּבוֹד   קָדוֹשׁ

אַשְׁרֵי

The **אַשְׁרֵי** is made of Psalm 145 and an introduction taken from other psalms (84.5, 114.15). It is in alphabetical order.

The **אַשְׁרֵי** is said three times a day. It is said twice during morning services as part of the *P'sukei d'Zimra*, the verses of song, and again after the **תְּפִלָּה** (*Amidah*). It is said for a third time at the beginning of the **מִנְחָה** (afternoon) service. When we say the **אַשְׁרֵי** as part of the Torah service on Shabbat we are actually beginning the *Mussaf* service (and replacing the weekday **אַשְׁרֵי** that came after the **תְּפִלָּה**). We do not say **אַשְׁרֵי** at evening services.

The Kabbalists explain why **אַשְׁרֵי** is not said at night: "**אַשְׁרֵי** is a prayer that thanks God for many things. The morning is the time when we feel really connected to our feelings of thanksgiving. As the day goes on our spirit is more directed toward just getting through the day. We say lots of prayers of thanksgiving at the beginning of the day. We have a long warmup for the service. In the afternoon these feelings are shrinking, and **אַשְׁרֵי** is the only preparation for **מִנְחָה**. By evening it is hard to find the **כַּוָּנָה** (spiritual focus) for joyful prayers of thanks. We save up our thanks for the next morning and just about jump into the **מַעֲרִיב**, the evening service" (Eli Munk, *The World of Prayer*, 195-6).

Question: Do people really tend to have different moods at different times of day? Does it make sense to adapt prayers to the time of day?

In this unit you will learn:
• About the **אַשְׁרֵי**.
• The root **י שׁ ב**

77

אַשְׁרֵי

1. אַשְׁרֵי יוֹשְׁבֵי בֵיתֶךָ	HAPPY are those who LIVE in Your HOUSE.
2. עוֹד יְהַלְלוּךָ סֶּלָה.	They are always HALELUing you. Selah (Psalm 84.5)!
3. אַשְׁרֵי הָעָם שֶׁכָּכָה לּוֹ	HAPPY are the PEOPLE for whom this is so.
4. אַשְׁרֵי הָעָם שֶׁיֵי אֱלֹהָיו.	HAPPY are the PEOPLE who have ADONAI as their GOD (Psalm 144.15).
5. תְּהִלָּה לְדָוִד.	A HALLELU by David
6. אֲרוֹמִמְךָ אֱלֹהַי הַמֶּלֶךְ,	I will LIFT YOU UP, my GOD the RULER
7. וַאֲבָרְכָה שִׁמְךָ לְעוֹלָם וָעֶד.	And I will BLESS Your NAME for ALWAYS and more.
8. בְּכָל-יוֹם אֲבָרְכֶךָ	Every day I will BLESS You
9. וַאֲהַלְלָה שִׁמְךָ לְעוֹלָם וָעֶד.	and HALLELU Your Name for ALWAYS and more.
10. גָּדוֹל יֵי וּמְהֻלָּל מְאֹד,	ADONAI is BIG and to be HALLELUed a lot.
11. וְלִגְדֻלָּתוֹ אֵין חֵקֶר.	God's BIGness can't be figured out.
12. דּוֹר לְדוֹר יְשַׁבַּח מַעֲשֶׂיךָ	Every generation praises Your DOINGS
13. וּגְבוּרֹתֶיךָ יַגִּידוּ.	and tells of Your HEROIC ACTIONS.
14. הֲדַר כְּבוֹד הוֹדֶךָ,	The majestic WEIGHT of Your SPLENDOR
15. וְדִבְרֵי נִפְלְאֹתֶיךָ אָשִׂיחָה.	and Your THINGS of WONDER I will tell.
16. וֶעֱזוּז נוֹרְאֹתֶיךָ יֹאמֵרוּ,	They will talk of Your AWESOME POWER
17. וּגְדֻלָּתְךָ אֲסַפְּרֶנָּה.	I will retell the GREAT THINGS You have done.
18. זֵכֶר רַב-טוּבְךָ יַבִּיעוּ	REMEMBERING the muchness of Your GOODNESS they will celebrate
19. וְצִדְקָתְךָ יְרַנֵּנוּ.	and Your acts of TZEDAKAH they will sing.
20. חַנּוּן וְרַחוּם יֵי,	ADONAI is GRACIOUS and MERCIFUL
21. אֶרֶךְ אַפַּיִם וּגְדָל-חָסֶד.	SLOW TO ANGER and GREAT in KINDNESS.
22. טוֹב יֵי לַכֹּל,	ADONAI is GOOD to all.
23. וְרַחֲמָיו עַל כָּל-מַעֲשָׂיו.	God showers MERCY on all God's creations.
24. יוֹדוּךָ יֵי כָּל-מַעֲשֶׂיךָ,	All Your works shall praise You, ADONAI
25. וַחֲסִידֶיךָ יְבָרְכוּכָה.	and Your HASIDIM shall bless You.

They will discuss the WEIGHT of Your EMPIRE	כְּבוֹד מַלְכוּתְךָ יֹאמֵרוּ, .26
and talk of Your HEROIC nature	וּגְבוּרָתְךָ יְדַבֵּרוּ. .27
to advertise to humanity God's HEROIC nature	לְהוֹדִיעַ לִבְנֵי הָאָדָם גְּבוּרֹתָיו, .28
and the WEIGHT and splendor of God's EMPIRE.	וּכְבוֹד הֲדַר מַלְכוּתוֹ. .29
Your EMPIRE is an EMPIRE that will last forever	מַלְכוּתְךָ מַלְכוּת כָּל־עֹלָמִים, .30
Your REGIME will last from GENERATION to GENERATION.	וּמֶמְשַׁלְתְּךָ בְּכָל־דּוֹר וָדֹר. .31
ADONAI LIFTS UP the fallen	סוֹמֵךְ יי לְכָל־הַנֹּפְלִים, .32
and STRAIGHTENS UP all who are bent over.	וְזוֹקֵף לְכָל־הַכְּפוּפִים. .33
All eyes look to You with HOPE	עֵינֵי כֹל אֵלֶיךָ יְשַׂבֵּרוּ, .34
and You give them their FOOD at the needed times.	וְאַתָּה נוֹתֵן לָהֶם אֶת־אָכְלָם בְּעִתּוֹ. .35
You OPEN Your HAND	פּוֹתֵחַ אֶת־יָדֶךָ, .36
and SATISFY the wants of all living things.	וּמַשְׂבִּיעַ לְכָל־חַי רָצוֹן. .37
ADONAI is a TZADDIK in every way	צַדִּיק יי בְּכָל־דְּרָכָיו, .38
and a HASID in every doing.	וְחָסִיד בְּכָל־מַעֲשָׂיו. .39
ADONAI is close to everyone who CALLS OUT	קָרוֹב יי לְכָל־קֹרְאָיו, .40
to all who CALL OUT in TRUTH.	לְכֹל אֲשֶׁר יִקְרָאֻהוּ בֶאֱמֶת. .41
GOD FULFILLS the WISHES of all who are in AWE	רְצוֹן יְרֵאָיו יַעֲשֶׂה, .42
God HEARS their cries and SAVES them.	וְאֶת־שַׁוְעָתָם יִשְׁמַע וְיוֹשִׁיעֵם. .43
ADONAI GUARDS all who love God	שׁוֹמֵר יי אֶת־כָּל־אֹהֲבָיו, .44
but DESTROYS all the wicked.	וְאֵת כָּל־הָרְשָׁעִים יַשְׁמִיד. .45
My mouth shall speak HALLELUYAHs for ADONAI	תְּהִלַּת יי יְדַבֶּר־פִּי, .46
and all flesh shall BLESS God's HOLY NAME	וִיבָרֵךְ כָּל־בָּשָׂר שֵׁם קָדְשׁוֹ .47
forever and beyond (Psalm 145).	לְעוֹלָם וָעֶד. .48
We will BLESS God	וַאֲנַחְנוּ נְבָרֵךְ יָהּ, .49
from this now to forever.	מֵעַתָּה וְעַד עוֹלָם .50
HALLELUYAH (Psalm 115.18).	הַלְלוּיָהּ. .51

Can you see the three letters יֹשֵׁב in these words?
Sometimes the י drops out.

בְּשִׁבְתְּךָ   יוֹשְׁבֵי   יָשַׁב

sat = יָשַׁב

those who sit/dwell = יוֹשְׁבֵי

in your sitting = בְּשִׁבְתְּךָ

Practice these phrases and circle all the words that contain the root יֹשֵׁב.

1. אַשְׁרֵי יוֹשְׁבֵי בֵיתֶךָ עוֹד יְהַלְלוּךָ סֶּלָה.

2. אֵל מֶלֶךְ יוֹשֵׁב עַל כִּסֵּא רַחֲמִים

3. וּמוֹשָׁב יְקָרוֹ בַּשָּׁמַיִם מִמַּעַל וּשְׁכִינַת עֻזּוֹ בְּגָבְהֵי מְרוֹמִים

4. אֲשֶׁר קִדְּשָׁנוּ בְּמִצְוֹתָיו וְצִוָּנוּ לֵישֵׁב בַּסֻּכָּה

5. וְשִׁנַּנְתָּם לְבָנֶיךָ וְדִבַּרְתָּ בָּם בְּשִׁבְתְּךָ בְּבֵיתֶךָ וּבְלֶכְתְּךָ בַדֶּרֶךְ

6. וַיֵּשֶׁב יי מֶלֶךְ לְעוֹלָם יי עֹז לְעַמּוֹ יִתֵּן יי יְבָרֵךְ אֶת עַמּוֹ בַשָּׁלוֹם

Write in the missing letters for these words that are built from the root יֹשֵׁב.

7. יוֹ__ __ב

8. וַיֵּשֶׁ__

9. לֵ__שֵׁב

10. __וֹשְׁבֵי

11. וּמוֹ__ב

12. בְּשִׁ__תְּךָ

80

Words

Happy! = אַשְׁרֵי
still = עוֹד
so be it = סֶלָה
nation = עַם
like that = שֶׁכָּכָה
God = אֱלֹהִים

הַלְלוּיָהּ   בַּיִת   יָשַׁב

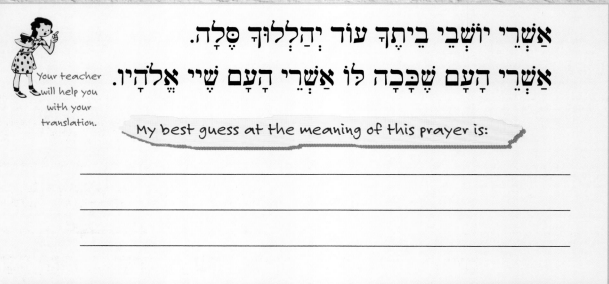

Your teacher will help you with your translation.

אַשְׁרֵי יוֹשְׁבֵי בֵיתֶךָ עוֹד יְהַלְלוּךָ סֶלָה.
אַשְׁרֵי הָעָם שֶׁכָּכָה לּוֹ אַשְׁרֵי הָעָם שֶׁיי אֱלֹהָיו.

My best guess at the meaning of this prayer is:

_____

_____

_____

Commentary

אַשְׁרֵי begins with a verse from Psalm 84, **אַשְׁרֵי יוֹשְׁבֵי בֵיתֶךָ**. Various commentators ask, "Which house is being talked about?"

The Temple. Just seeing it was enough to inspire people (Radak).

The Synagogue. This refers to people who can get themselves into a deep prayer state (*Brakhot* 32a).

God's throne room. In a deep state of prayer, people can get close to God (Rabbenu Yonah).

Questions
1. Which answer do you like best?
2. What is your understanding of this phrase?

עֲצֹר!

Another Alphabetical Prayer

Practice this prayer (also in alphabetical order), which is part of the Shabbat morning יוֹצֵר אוֹר.

1. אֵל אָדוֹן עַל כָּל-הַמַּעֲשִׂים

2. בָּרוּךְ וּמְבֹרָךְ בְּפִי כָּל-נְשָׁמָה

3. גָּדְלוֹ וְטוּבוֹ מָלֵא עוֹלָם

4. דַּעַת וּתְבוּנָה סוֹבְבִים אוֹתוֹ

5. הַמִּתְגָּאֶה עַל חַיּוֹת הַקֹּדֶשׁ

6. וְנֶהְדָּר בְּכָבוֹד עַל הַמֶּרְכָּבָה

7. זְכוּת וּמִישׁוֹר לִפְנֵי כִסְאוֹ

8. חֶסֶד וְרַחֲמִים לִפְנֵי כְבוֹדוֹ

9. טוֹבִים מְאוֹרוֹת שֶׁבָּרָא אֱלֹהֵינוּ

10. יְצָרָם בְּדַעַת בְּבִינָה וּבְהַשְׂכֵּל

11. כֹּחַ וּגְבוּרָה נָתַן בָּהֶם

12. לִהְיוֹת מוֹשְׁלִים בְּקֶרֶב תֵּבֵל

13. מְלֵאִים זִיו וּמְפִיקִים נֹגַהּ

14. נָאֶה זִיוָם בְּכָל-הָעוֹלָם

15. שְׂמֵחִים בְּצֵאתָם וְשָׂשִׂים בְּבוֹאָם

16. עוֹשִׂים בְּאֵימָה רְצוֹן קוֹנָם

17. פְּאֵר וְכָבוֹד נוֹתְנִים לִשְׁמוֹ

18. צָהֳלָה וְרִנָּה לְזֵכֶר מַלְכוּתוֹ

19. קָרָא לַשֶּׁמֶשׁ וַיִּזְרַח אוֹר

20. רָאָה וְהִתְקִין צוּרַת הַלְּבָנָה

21. שֶׁבַח נוֹתְנִים לוֹ כָּל-צְבָא מָרוֹם

22. תִּפְאֶרֶת וּגְדֻלָּה שְׂרָפִים וְאוֹפַנִּים וְחַיּוֹת הַקֹּדֶשׁ

The Alef-Bet of Creation

God was ready to create the world. The letters of the *Alef-Bet* gathered around. Each wanted to be chosen as the beginning of the first word that God would speak that would begin the process of creation.

First came ת. It suggested that תּוֹרָה would be the perfect first word. But God rejected ת, saying, "You also end the word מֵת (death)."

Next came שׁ, who tried שָׂמֵחַ (happy), but God countered with שִׂנְאָה (hatred).

ר said רַחֲמִים (mercy), but God said, רַע (evil).

So it went from letter to letter.

ג suggested גָּדוֹל (big). God replied גָּלוּת (exile).

Finally ב said בָּרוּךְ. God said, "Yes. I will use you to begin בְּרֵאשִׁית."

Then God saw the א. א had been silent. א never says anything. God said, "If only you had spoken up, I would have created the world through you. But to reward your humility I will begin the Ten Commandments with you." They begin אָנֹכִי יי אֱלֹהֶיךָ.

Questions

1. What lesson(s) can you learn from this story?
2. What does this story teach you about the א-ב?
3. How can knowing this story help you know where to point your heart when you say the אַשְׁרֵי?

all = כֹּל
mercy = רַחֲמִים
give thanks = יָדָה

Word Parts

to/for = לְ
the = הַ
and = וְ/וּ
His = ◌ָיו
Your = ◌ֶיךָ

בָּרוּךְ   חֶסֶד   עָשָׂה   טוֹב

Your teacher will help you with your translation.

טוֹב יי לַכֹּל, וְרַחֲמָיו עַל כָּל-מַעֲשָׂיו.

יוֹדוּךָ יי כָּל-מַעֲשֶׂיךָ, וַחֲסִידֶיךָ יְבָרְכוּכָה.

My best guess at the meaning of this prayer is:

_____

_____

_____

Showering Mercy

The ט-verse in the אַשְׁרֵי says:

טוֹב יי לַכֹּל, וְרַחֲמָיו
עַל כָּל-מַעֲשָׂיו

"ADONAI is GOOD to all. God showers MERCY on all God's creations." The Midrash tells a story about it.

Once there was a drought. Rabbi Tanhuma told everyone to fast and say prayers of repentance. They had a mini-Yom Kippur, but still no rain came. Rabbi Tanhuma said to everyone, "If you have compassion for each other, then God will have compassion for you." The people of the town took him seriously and were better to each other.

כָּפוּף   זוֹקֵף   נוֹפֵל   סוֹמֵךְ

Your teacher will help you with your translation.

סוֹמֵךְ יי לְכָל-הַנֹּפְלִים, וְזוֹקֵף לְכָל-הַכְּפוּפִים.

My best guess at the meaning of this prayer is:

_____

_____

_____

The next day those people who were distributing food to the poor saw Mordechai. Mordechai was giving money to his ex-wife. Everyone assumed that he was cheating on his new wife by spending time with his ex-wife. They saw the money that changed hands as evidence of adultery. Rabbi Tanḥuma sent for Mordechai. He asked him about what had been seen. Mordechai said, "I gave money to my former wife because she was not doing well. Her second husband had died, and she was now very poor. I listened to your words, had compassion on her, and helped her out."

Rabbi Tanḥuma prayed, "Ruler of the Cosmos, just as this man who had no obligation to support this woman behaved compassionately toward her, You, the All-Compassionate One, should take care of Abraham, Sarah, Isaac, Rebekkah, Jacob, Leah and Rachel's children, Your children." It began to rain (*B.R. 33*).

Questions

1. What does this story teach us about God?
2. What does this story teach us about the letter ט? What does it teach us about all the letters?
3. How can knowing this story help you know where to point your heart when you say the אַשְׁרֵי?

In the Talmud we are told that anyone who says the אַשְׁרֵי three times a day will earn a place in עוֹלָם הַבָּא (the reality to come). To make this likely the rabbis built it into daily services three times. In the Talmud they ask, "What makes this psalm (and this prayer) so important that just by saying it enough one gets a great future?" The Talmud gives two answers:

1. Because each line of this psalm begins with a different letter of the Hebrew Alef-Bet—going from the first letter א to the last letter ת. Every letter includes everything.

2. There is no verse for the Hebrew letter נ in אַשְׁרֵי. But that letter shows up as part of the word נוֹפְלִים (fallen) when the psalm says "God lifts up all the fallen." This teaches that when we follow God's example, we will be lifted up, too (*Brakhot* 4b).

Questions

1. Why is a prayer that uses every letter in the א־ב a path to spiritual success?
2. What lesson can we learn from the missing letter נ?
3. How can knowing this story help you know where to point your heart when you say the אַשְׁרֵי?

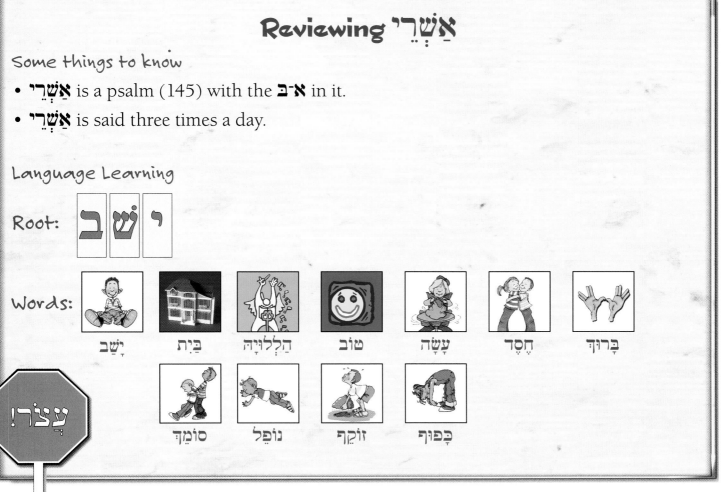

Reviewing אַשְׁרֵי

Some things to know

- אַשְׁרֵי is a psalm (145) with the א־ב in it.
- אַשְׁרֵי is said three times a day.

Language Learning

Root: ב שׁ י

Words:

יָשַׁב | בַּיִת | הַלְלוּיָהּ | טוֹב | עָשָׂה | חֶסֶד | בָּרוּךְ

סוֹמֵךְ | נוֹפֵל | זוֹקֵף | כְּפוּף

עֲצֹר!

Unit 10 Returning the Torah to the Ark

The Torah service ends by revisiting the metaphors we used to begin.

- When we took out the Torah we started by lifting the Ark that led us through the wilderness.
- We remembered when David brought the Ark up to Jerusalem.
- We visited Mt. Sinai and recalled hearing Torah through Moses and remembered hearing Torah directly from God.
- We had an experience of feeling close to God.

When we stand for the Torah service we return to Mt. Sinai because the Jews stood as the Torah was given.

הוֹדוּ עַל אֶרֶץ and יְהַלְלוּ

These two prayers are like the **בָּרְכוּ**. The leader invites the congregation to praise, and they join in. These verses come from Psalm 148, which gives us images of what the world will be like when the Torah has finished its job and the messianic era has come.

מִזְמוֹר לְדָוִד

Psalm 29 begins a Torah parade in many synagogues. This psalm echoes the words reported in 1 Chronicles 16.28-9 that David sang as he moved the Ark to its permanent place in the Temple (Ha-Mikra v'ha-Mesorah).

וּבְנֻחֹה יֹאמַר

This paragraph is made up of a number of biblical verses strung together to connect two themes, the resting of the Ark in the wilderness (which parallels the return of the Torah to our ark) and the return of the relationship between God and Israel (that is what we hope the reading of Torah will accomplish). **עֵץ חַיִּים הִיא** (It is a tree of life) and **הֲשִׁיבֵנוּ** (Return us) are part of this second part. The Reform movement skips the first part of this paragraph.

In this unit you will learn:

- About returning the Torah to the Ark.

- Roots ק ח ז and שׁ ו ב

87

Returning the Torah to the Ark

HALLELUYAH the Eternal's NAME	יְהַלְלוּ אֶת־שֵׁם יי .1
because God's NAME alone will stand out.	כִּי נִשְׂגָּב שְׁמוֹ לְבַדּוֹ. .2
God's GLORY is above earth and heaven	הוֹדוֹ עַל אֶרֶץ וְשָׁמָיִם .4
God will lift up the PRIDE of God's people	וַיָּרֶם קֶרֶן לְעַמּוֹ .5
Causing a HALLELUYAH for the Committed-Ones	תְּהִלָּה לְכָל־חֲסִידָיו .6
For the Families-of-Israel, God's Close People.	לִבְנֵי יִשְׂרָאֵל עַם קְרֹבוֹ. .7
HALLELUYAH! (Psalm 148.13-14)	הַלְלוּיָהּ. .8
And when the ark RESTED he would say:	וּבְנֻחֹה יֹאמַר .9
"ETERNAL, RETURN to the many thousands of Israel" (Numbers 10.36).	שׁוּבָה יי רִבְבוֹת אַלְפֵי יִשְׂרָאֵל .10
"ETERNAL, RISE to your RESTING.	קוּמָה יי לִמְנוּחָתֶךָ .11
You and the Ark of Your Strength.	אַתָּה וַאֲרוֹן עֻזֶּךָ. .12
Let Your Kohanim be dressed as TZADIKIM	כֹּהֲנֶיךָ יִלְבְּשׁוּ־צֶדֶק .13
Let Your HASIDIM sing joyously	וַחֲסִידֶיךָ יְרַנֵּנוּ. .14
For the sake of DAVID, Your Servant	בַּעֲבוּר דָּוִד עַבְדֶּךָ .15
Don't TURN AWAY the face of Your MESSIAH (Psalm 132.8-10).	אַל תָּשֵׁב פְּנֵי מְשִׁיחֶךָ. .16
For I have given you a GOOD TEACHING	כִּי לֶקַח טוֹב נָתַתִּי לָכֶם .17
MY TORAH, do not abandon it (Proverbs 4.2).	תּוֹרָתִי אַל תַּעֲזֹבוּ. .18
It is a TREE-of-LIFE	עֵץ חַיִּים הִיא .19
to those who STRONGLY HOLD it	לַמַּחֲזִיקִים בָּהּ .20
and those who are SUPPORTED by it are HAPPY (Proverbs 3.18).	וְתוֹמְכֶיהָ מְאֻשָּׁר. .21
Its PATHS are good PATHS	דְּרָכֶיהָ דַרְכֵי־נֹעַם .22
and all its WAYS lead to PEACE… (Proverbs 3.17).	וְכָל־נְתִיבוֹתֶיהָ שָׁלוֹם. .23
RETURN US to You ADONAI and we will RETURN	הֲשִׁיבֵנוּ יי אֵלֶיךָ וְנָשׁוּבָה .24
RENEW our days as of old (Lamentations 5.21).	חַדֵּשׁ יָמֵינוּ כְּקֶדֶם. .25

Can you see the letters שֵׁם in these words?

my name = שְׁמִי	name = שֵׁם
your name (female) = שְׁמֵךְ	your name (male) = שִׁמְךָ
her name = שְׁמָהּ	his name = שְׁמוֹ

Practice these phrases and circle all the words that contain שֵׁם.

1. יְהַלְלוּ אֶת־שֵׁם יי כִּי נִשְׂגָּב שְׁמוֹ לְבַדּוֹ

2. הַלְלוּ עַבְדֵי יי הַלְלוּ אֶת־שֵׁם יי

3. יְהִי שֵׁם יי מְבֹרָךְ מֵעַתָּה וְעַד עוֹלָם

4. וִיבָרֵךְ כָּל־בָּשָׂר שֵׁם קָדְשׁוֹ לְעוֹלָם וָעֶד

5. אֲרוֹמִמְךָ אֱלֹהַי הַמֶּלֶךְ וַאֲבָרְכָה שִׁמְךָ לְעוֹלָם וָעֶד

6. נְקַדֵּשׁ אֶת שִׁמְךָ בָּעוֹלָם כְּשֵׁם שֶׁמַּקְדִּישִׁים אוֹתוֹ בִּשְׁמֵי מָרוֹם

7. וְהָיָה יי לְמֶלֶךְ עַל כָּל־הָאָרֶץ בַּיּוֹם הַהוּא יִהְיֶה יי אֶחָד וּשְׁמוֹ אֶחָד

Which word means...

your name (female)_____   his name_____

my name_____   her name_____

your name (male)_____

שְׁמִי שֵׁם שִׁמְךָ שְׁמֵךְ שְׁמָהּ שְׁמוֹ

89

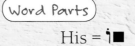

הַלֵּל

Your teacher will help you with your translation.

יְהַלְלוּ אֶת־שֵׁם יי כִּי נִשְׂגָּב שְׁמוֹ לְבַדּוֹ.

My best guess at the meaning of this prayer is:

_____

_____

_____

Commentary

יְהַלְלוּ comes from Psalm 148. Jewish commentators believe that this psalm speaks of the time of the messianic era.

The psalmist eagerly anticipates the day when Jerusalem will be rebuilt and from it the whole universe will be repaired. At that time "God will be praised from the heavens, from the highest heights." (That is the idea expressed in the first verse.) (Rabbi Avraham Chaim Feuer, *ArtScroll commentary on Psalms*)

Question

Why is it important for the final Torah parade to begin with a Messianic image?

עֲצֹר!

Can you see the three letters חזק in these words?

לַמַּחֲזִיקִים   נִתְחַזֵּק   חָזָק

strong = חָזָק

we will be strengthened = נִתְחַזֵּק

to those who hold strongly = לַמַּחֲזִיקִים

Practice these phrases and circle all the words that contain the root חזק.

2. כִּי גוֹאֵל חָזָק אַתָּה   1. וְגָאֲלוֹ מִיַּד חָזָק מִמֶּנּוּ

4. כִּי חִזַּק בְּרִיחֵי שְׁעָרָיִךְ   3. וּבְיָדְךָ לְגַדֵּל וּלְחַזֵּק לַכֹּל

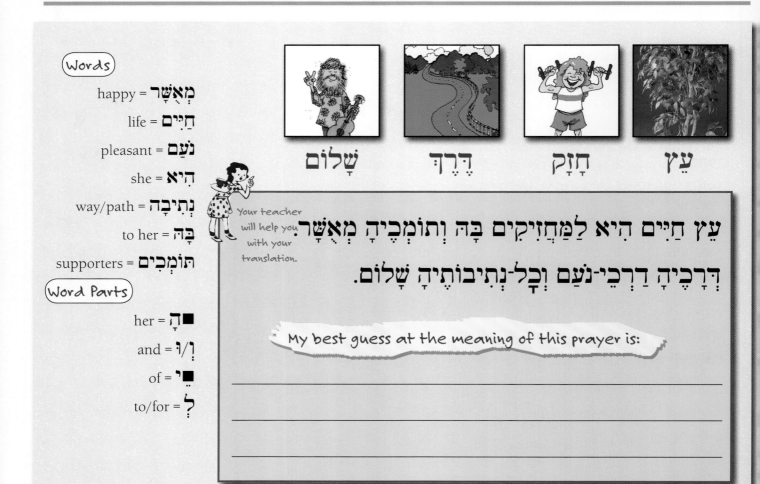

(Words)

happy = מְאֻשָּׁר

life = חַיִּים

pleasant = נֹעַם

she = הִיא

way/path = נְתִיבָה

to her = בָּה

supporters = תוֹמְכִים

(Word Parts)

her = הָ■

and = וְ/וּ

of = ■ֵי

to/for = לְ

שָׁלוֹם   דֶּרֶךְ   חָזָק   עֵץ

Your teacher will help you with your translation.

עֵץ חַיִּים הִיא לַמַּחֲזִיקִים בָּהּ וְתֹמְכֶיהָ מְאֻשָּׁר. דְּרָכֶיהָ דַרְכֵי־נֹעַם וְכָל־נְתִיבֹתֶיהָ שָׁלוֹם.

My best guess at the meaning of this prayer is:

_____

_____

_____

The Torah Is a Tree of Life

God hid the tree that gave eternal life to those who ate from it and in its place God gave us the Torah.

We know this because it says,

"It is a tree of life to those who hold fast to it"
   (Proverbs 3.18).

When a person studies it and sees God's wisdom in it,

and God's righteousness,

and God's just laws and statutes,

that person can be brought into a new state of mind.

When a person does this it comes with reward in
   this world and reward in the next world.

We know this because it says,

"The Eternal commanded us to observe
   all these laws

for our lasting good and to grant us
   life" (Deuteronomy 6.24).

Midrash ha-Gadol, Bereshit 3.24

Questions

1. In what ways is the Torah like the Tree of Life (in the Garden of Eden)?
2. How does the Torah give us life and eternal life? (What do you mean by eternal life?)
3. How can remembering this midrash help you point your heart when you say or sing עֵץ חַיִּים הִיא?

Archik's Torah

During the Russian Revolution it was often hard to get food. Students at the Chofetz Chayim's yeshiva were starving. One Shabbat afternoon on the way home from services the Chofetz Chayim ran into Archik. Archik had been a yeshiva student, but he was now a communist and the local government official.

The Chofetz Chayim said "*Gut Shabbas*" to him. He said, "Saturday is like any other day to me." "Good enough, because all days come from God," the Chofetz Chayim answered. Archik smiled, and the two of them talked for a while. Finally the rabbi asked him, "Would you like to hear a good piece of Torah?" The communist said, "No, thank you." "How about a good saying?" was the next question. "Why not?" was Archik's answer.

The Chofetz Chayim said, "God put the Tree of Life in the middle of the garden and not on a side so that every person can have equal access. Every person can get to the Tree of Life in his or her own way. Some do it through studying Torah. Some do it through good deeds. Some do it through the strength of their heart. You could get to the Tree of Life, you could win a place in the עוֹלָם הַבָּא (the next world), by selling us a little food."

After Havdalah, as they were wishing each other "*Shavua Tov*" (a good week) at the end of Shabbat, a wagon arrived at the yeshiva filled with flour and other foods.

Questions

1. Archik had rejected Judaism when he became a communist. Why do you think he helped out the Chofetz Chayim and his students?
2. Where is the Tree of Life in this story? Who was doing the "holding fast"?
3. How can knowing this story help you point your heart when singing עֵץ חַיִּים הִיא as the סֵפֶר תּוֹרָה is being put away?

עֲצֹר!

Can you see the three letters שוב in these words?

הֲשִׁיבֵנוּ   תְּשׁוּבָה   שׁוּב

שׁוּב = turn

תְּשׁוּבָה = repentence

הֲשִׁיבֵנוּ = return us

Practice these phrases and circle all the words that contain the root שוב.

1. בָּרוּךְ אַתָּה יי הָרוֹצֶה בִּתְשׁוּבָה

2. וְהָשֵׁב אֶת־הָעֲבוֹדָה לִדְבִיר בֵּיתֶךָ

3. הֲשִׁיבֵנוּ יי אֵלֶיךָ וְנָשׁוּבָה חַדֵּשׁ יָמֵינוּ כְּקֶדֶם.

4. וְתֶחֱזֶינָה עֵינֵינוּ בְּשׁוּבְךָ לְצִיּוֹן בְּרַחֲמִים

5. הֲשִׁיבֵנוּ אָבִינוּ לְתוֹרָתֶךָ וְקָרְבֵנוּ מַלְכֵּנוּ לַעֲבוֹדָתֶךָ

6. הָשִׁיבָה שׁוֹפְטֵינוּ כְּבָרִאשׁוֹנָה וְיוֹעֲצֵינוּ כְּבַתְּחִלָּה

7. אָבִינוּ מַלְכֵּנוּ הַחֲזִירֵנוּ בִּתְשׁוּבָה שְׁלֵמָה לְפָנֶיךָ

8. שִׁיר הַמַּעֲלוֹת בְּשׁוּב יי אֶת־שִׁיבַת צִיּוֹן הָיִינוּ כְּחֹלְמִים

9. וּבְנֻחֹה יֹאמַר שׁוּבָה יי רִבְבוֹת אַלְפֵי יִשְׂרָאֵל

10. שׁוּבָה יי אֶת־שְׁבִיתֵנוּ כַּאֲפִיקִים בַּנֶּגֶב הַזֹּרְעִים בְּדִמְעָה בְּרִנָּה יִקְצֹרוּ

Words

to = אֶל

renew = חַדֵּשׁ

before = קֶדֶם

Word Parts

us/our = נוּ■

your = ךָ■

and = וְ/וּ

like/as = כְּ

יוֹם

שׁוּב

Your teacher will help you with your translation.

הֲשִׁיבֵנוּ יי אֵלֶיךָ וְנָשׁוּבָה חַדֵּשׁ יָמֵינוּ כְּקֶדֶם

My best guess at the meaning of this prayer is:

_____

_____

_____

The Seven Shepherds

One Shabbat Rabbi Isaac Luria, the holy Ari, told his students, "If you can keep from saying a word other than the prayers, and if you can keep from laughing, I will call the seven shepherds to read from the Torah." All of the students knew who the shepherds were and readily agreed. They prayed with great intensity. When it came time to read the Torah, the Ari called Aaron, the first high priest, for the first עֲלִיָה. Aaron said the blessings and read from the Torah. Aaron had been a shepherd of sheep and a shepherd of people. Moses was called for the next עֲלִיָה. He, too, had been a shepherd. Abraham, Isaac, Jacob, and Joseph were called for the next four עֲלִיוֹת. For the seventh עֲלִיָה the Holy Ari called King David. He came from the back of the synagogue. He was dancing and

jumping and singing. He was filled with spirit and energy. One of the students laughed with joy. It broke the moment. David vanished. The Ari came to the בִּימָה and took the final עֲלִיָּה. It was quiet and sad. All knew that the Messiah would have been the מַפְטִיר, the one to read the הַפְטָרָה (*Hemdat ha-Yamin, Shabbat* 81a).

Questions

1. How does the past help us to build the future?
2. What was the importance of the seven shepherds in this story?
3. How did the laughter destroy the moment?
4. What does it mean to "renew our days as of old"?
5. How does knowing this story help you to point your heart when you say הֲשִׁיבֵנוּ?

Reviewing "Returning the Torah to the Ark"

Some things to know

- This service has three big images: moving the ark in the wilderness, returning the ark to Jerusalem, and remembering Mt. Sinai.
- When we put the Torah away we echo the way we took it out, with a parade and with a ceremony.

Language Learning

Roots: and

Words:

                        and

הַלֵּל   עֵץ   דֶּרֶךְ   שָׁלוֹם   יוֹם   שׁוּב   and   שֵׁם

עֲצֹר!

אֵין כֵּאלֹהֵינוּ

In this unit you will learn:
- About the אֵין כֵּאלֹהֵינוּ.
- About the 100 Blessing Code

אֵין כֵּאלֹהֵינוּ is a hymn, a song that is sung near the end of the service. In the traditional pattern (also found in Conservative services) it comes after the מוּסָף (additional) service. Reform synagogues do not have מוּסָף, and they often use it as a closing hymn.

In Sefardic (and Hasidic) services אֵין כֵּאלֹהֵינוּ is said every morning. In the Ashkenazic tradition it is said only on Shabbat. Sefardic Jews are Jews who come from countries with dominant Islamic influence. Ashkenazic Jews come from countries with dominant Christian influence. Spain had both influences, and "Sefardic" comes from the Hebrew word for Spain.

אֵין כֵּאלֹהֵינוּ Math

It is a mitzvah to say 100 בְּרָכוֹת a day. The Shabbat עֲמִידָה has only seven, while the weekday עֲמִידָה has 18. That leaves us eleven short for each of three services, or a total of thirty-three. The מוּסָף service with its עֲמִידָה makes up seven of them. We still need twenty-six. Six of them come in the blessings for the "extra" third meal on Shabbat afternoon. The other twenty are taken from the twenty times we mention God directly in this prayer (four names times five verses). In addition we have אַתָּה, בָּרוּך, and even אָמֵן. Amen comes from the verses that begin אֵין, מִי and נוֹדֶה (Rashi's Siddur).

The Spice Connection

The last verse of אֵין כֵּאלֹהֵינוּ (not usually said in Reform congregations) talks about the spices burned as incense in the Temple. This is followed in the traditional siddur by a paragraph from the Talmud that gives the formula for the incense. We are told two interesting things about that incense. First, that by just listing its formula we are given credit for fulfilling the mitzvah of burning it (*Darkhei Moshe on Tur* 233). Second, that prayers go up to heaven just like incense (Psalm 141.2).

אֵין כֵּאלֹהֵינוּ

No ONE is like OUR GOD.	אֵין כֵּאלֹהֵינוּ	1.
No ONE is like OUR ETERNAL.	אֵין כַּאדוֹנֵינוּ	2.
No ONE is like OUR RULER.	אֵין כְּמַלְכֵּנוּ	3.
No ONE is like OUR RESCUER.	אֵין כְּמוֹשִׁיעֵנוּ.	4.
WHO is like OUR GOD?	מִי כֵאלֹהֵינוּ	5.
WHO is like OUR ETERNAL?	מִי כַאדוֹנֵינוּ	6.
WHO is like OUR RULER?	מִי כְמַלְכֵּנוּ	7.
WHO is like OUR RESCUER?	מִי כְמוֹשִׁיעֵנוּ.	8.
Let us THANK OUR GOD.	נוֹדֶה לֵאלֹהֵינוּ	9.
Let us THANK OUR ETERNAL.	נוֹדֶה לַאדוֹנֵינוּ	10.
Let us THANK OUR RULER.	נוֹדֶה לְמַלְכֵּנוּ	11.
Let us THANK OUR RESCUER.	נוֹדֶה לְמוֹשִׁיעֵנוּ.	12.
BLESS OUR GOD.	בָּרוּךְ אֱלֹהֵינוּ	13.
BLESS OUR ETERNAL.	בָּרוּךְ אֲדוֹנֵינוּ	14.
BLESS OUR RULER.	בָּרוּךְ מַלְכֵּנוּ	15.
BLESS OUR RESCUER.	בָּרוּךְ מוֹשִׁיעֵנוּ.	16.
YOU are OUR GOD.	אַתָּה הוּא אֱלֹהֵינוּ	17.
YOU are OUR ETERNAL.	אַתָּה הוּא אֲדוֹנֵינוּ	18.
YOU are OUR RULER.	אַתָּה הוּא מַלְכֵּנוּ	19.
YOU are OUR RESCUER.	אַתָּה הוּא מוֹשִׁיעֵנוּ.	20.
You are the ONE before Whom our ancestors	אַתָּה הוּא שֶׁהִקְטִירוּ אֲבוֹתֵינוּ	21.
BURNED the fragrant incense.	לְפָנֶיךָ אֶת-קְטֹרֶת הַסַּמִּים.	22.

The traditional siddur has many passages about the Temple and our desire to have another one. The Reform siddur has cut out all (or just about all) references to the Temple, stating that we have no desire to have another Temple. The Conservative Movement keeps most of the Temple passages but usually explains them as metaphors and not the hope for a new Temple.

Questions: What is the good part of keeping the "Temple parts"? What is the good part of taking out the "Temple parts"? What do you do in your synagogue?

The Incense Offering

Every one of the *Kohanim* (priests) wanted to be the one to offer the incense offering in the Temple. The incense offering was burnt over fire, and a cloud of smoke rose up toward the heavens, up to God. No one ever got to do it twice, because everyone wanted to do it. It was believed that making this offering would make you rich *(Yoma 26a)*.

There is a rule in the Torah that the formula for the incense could be used only in the Temple. No one could practice making it. No one could make it for his or her own use. One family in Jerusalem used to mix all of the spices for the incense in the Temple. They taught the secret to no one. To prove that they were not using the formula to their own advantage, none of them ever wore perfume, not even at their weddings *(Kritot 5)*.

Questions

1. Why do you think it was important to smell the incense only in the Temple? (This answer is not given in the Torah or Talmud.)
2. What in your life is an honor like offering the incense, something you can do only once and that makes you rich?
3. In what way did a *kohen* become rich by offering the incense? (Hint: Not all riches are money.)
4. How can knowing about the incense help you to point your heart when you sing אֵין כֵּאלֹהֵינוּ?

Fill in the Missing Translation of אֵין כֵּאלֹהֵינוּ

No
one is   like
our God   No
one is   like
our Eternal

אֵין כְּמוֹשִׁיעֵנוּ. אֵין כְּמַלְכֵּנוּ,

like
our Ruler   _____   like
our Rescuer

אֵין כַּאדוֹנֵינוּ, אֵין כֵּאלֹהֵינוּ,

who
is   _____   who
is   like
our Eternal

מִי כַאדוֹנֵינוּ, מִי כֵאלֹהֵינוּ,

who
is   _____   _____   like
our Rescuer

מִי כְמוֹשִׁיעֵנוּ. מִי כְמַלְכֵּנוּ,

Let us
give
thanks   to our
God   Let us
give
thanks   _____

נוֹדֶה לַאדוֹנֵינוּ, נוֹדֶה לֵאלֹהֵינוּ,

נוֹדֶה לְמוֹשִׁיעֵנוּ. נוֹדֶה לְמַלְכֵּנוּ,

Bless   _____   Bless

בָּרוּךְ אֲדוֹנֵינוּ, בָּרוּךְ אֱלֹהֵינוּ,

בָּרוּךְ מוֹשִׁיעֵנוּ. בָּרוּךְ מַלְכֵּנוּ,

You are   _____   _____

אַתָּה הוּא אֲדוֹנֵינוּ, אַתָּה הוּא אֱלֹהֵינוּ,

אַתָּה הוּא מוֹשִׁיעֵנוּ. אַתָּה הוּא מַלְכֵּנוּ,

עֲצֹר!

Unit 12 — עָלֵינוּ

עָלֵינוּ is a prayer with a history:

- There is a memory that Joshua first said עָלֵינוּ after the Families-of-Israel defeated the city of Jericho. When "the walls came tumbling down," Joshua knew that God was the Ruler and the One Who deserves praise (*Kol Bo,* Rav Hai Gaon, *Shaarei Teshuvah,* 43).

- There is another memory that Rav, a Babylonian rabbi from the third century, wrote the עָלֵינוּ or reclaimed עָלֵינוּ, and made it part of the מוּסָף service on Rosh ha-Shanah. There it was used to introduce the theme of God as Ruler and us as subject to God's rule (*Otzar Ha-Tefilah, Iyun Tefilah*).

- In 1171, during the persecution of the Jews of Blois, France, thirty-four Jewish men and seventeen Jewish women, falsely accused of ritual murder, died as martyrs at the stake. An eyewitness wrote to Rabbi Jacob of Orleans, "Their death was accompanied by a mysterious song, resounding through the stillness of the night. It caused the gentiles who heard it from a distance to wonder at the melodious strains, the likes of which had never before been heard. The martyrs had sung עָלֵינוּ as their dying prayer" (Yosef ha-Kohen, *Emek ha-Bakha* "Valley of Tears").

- By the 1400s the עָלֵינוּ had become one of the concluding prayers of every service, probably because of the memory of the way that martyrs used it as a song of faith.

- At the turn of the fifteenth century Pesach Peter, an apostate Jew, spread the lie that part of the עָלֵינוּ was used to slur Christianity.

- Today עָלֵינוּ is one of the prayers that is most changed in various editions of the siddur.

Rabbi Joel Sirkes wrote, "עָלֵינוּ is a theological summary at the end of the service reminding us of God's unity and the ultimate goal of eradicating idolatry."

In this unit you will learn:

- The history of עָלֵינוּ: Joshua, Rav, and Blois.
- Aleinu as a "theological summary."

עָלֵינוּ

English	Hebrew	№
It is our job to praise the MASTER-of-All	עָלֵינוּ לְשַׁבֵּחַ לַאֲדוֹן הַכֹּל,	1
To grant GREATness	לָתֵת גְּדֻלָּה	2
to the ONE-Who-Stages CREATION,	לְיוֹצֵר בְּרֵאשִׁית,	2
The ONE-Who-Didn't-Make-Us	שֶׁלֹּא עָשָׂנוּ	4
like the other NATIONS-of-the-LANDS	כְּגוֹיֵי הָאֲרָצוֹת	5
and didn't PUT our fate	וְלֹא שָׂמָנוּ	6
with the other FAMILIES-of-the-EARTH	כְּמִשְׁפְּחוֹת הָאֲדָמָה,	7
and did not PUT our PORTION with theirs.	שֶׁלֹּא שָׂם חֶלְקֵנוּ כָּהֶם	8
and our LOT with the MANY.	וְגוֹרָלֵנוּ כְּכָל־הֲמוֹנָם.	9
The One Who GAVE us the Torah of truth	*שֶׁנָּתַן לָנוּ תּוֹרַת אֱמֶת	
and planted eternal life within us.	וְחַיֵּי עוֹלָם נָטַע בְּתוֹכֵנוּ.	
We BOW & BEND & FLATTEN-in-THANKS	וַאֲנַחְנוּ כּוֹרְעִים וּמִשְׁתַּחֲוִים וּמוֹדִים	10
Before the RULER-of-RULERS	לִפְנֵי מֶלֶךְ מַלְכֵי הַמְּלָכִים	11
The HOLY ONE-Who-is-to-be-BLESSED.	הַקָּדוֹשׁ בָּרוּךְ הוּא.	12
The ONE-WHO-Spread-out the HEAVENS	שֶׁהוּא נוֹטֶה שָׁמַיִם	13
and laid the earth's foundations	וְיוֹסֵד אָרֶץ,	14
and has the SEAT-of-Homage in the heavens above	וּמוֹשַׁב יְקָרוֹ בַּשָּׁמַיִם מִמַּעַל	15
and the NEIGHBORHOOD-of-Power in the highest heights.	וּשְׁכִינַת עֻזּוֹ בְּגָבְהֵי מְרוֹמִים.	16
God is our God—there is none other.	הוּא אֱלֹהֵינוּ, אֵין עוֹד.	17
In TRUTH God is RULER—NOTHING compares	אֱמֶת מַלְכֵּנוּ, אֶפֶס זוּלָתוֹ,	18
as it is WRITTEN:	כַּכָּתוּב בְּתוֹרָתוֹ:	19
"And You are to KNOW today in the thoughts of your HEART,	וְיָדַעְתָּ הַיּוֹם וַהֲשֵׁבֹתָ אֶל לְבָבֶךָ,	20
that ADONAI is the ONE God	כִּי יי הוּא הָאֱלֹהִים	21
both in HEAVEN ABOVE and on EARTH below—	בַּשָּׁמַיִם מִמַּעַל וְעַל הָאָרֶץ מִתָּחַת,	22
NONE can COMPARE" (Deuteronomy 4.39).	אֵין עוֹד.	23

BECAUSE of this, we WISH from You	עַל כֵּן נְקַוֶּה לְּךָ 24.
ADONAI, our God,	יי אֱלֹהֵינוּ 25.
To soon SEE the WONDER of your strength	לִרְאוֹת מְהֵרָה בְּתִפְאֶרֶת עֻזֶּךָ, 26.
to terminate idolatry from the earth	לְהַעֲבִיר גִּלּוּלִים מִן הָאָרֶץ 27.
and completely cut off the false gods—	וְהָאֱלִילִים כָּרוֹת יִכָּרֵתוּן. 28.
to do TIKKUN OLAM in God's EMPIRE	לְתַקֵּן עוֹלָם בְּמַלְכוּת שַׁדַּי 29.
and all humanity will CALL Your NAME	וְכָל־בְּנֵי בָשָׂר יִקְרְאוּ בִשְׁמֶךָ, 30.
to RETURN to You	לְהַפְנוֹת אֵלֶיךָ 31.
all the WICKED-of-the-EARTH.	כָּל־רִשְׁעֵי אָרֶץ. 32.
All the inhabitants of the world will REALIZE and KNOW	יַכִּירוּ וְיֵדְעוּ כָּל־יוֹשְׁבֵי תֵבֵל 33.
that every KNEE must BEND to YOU	כִּי לְךָ תִּכְרַע כָּל־בֶּרֶךְ, 34.
and every TONGUE must SWEAR allegiance to You (Isaiah 45.23).	תִּשָּׁבַע כָּל־לָשׁוֹן. 35.
Before You ADONAI, our God,	לְפָנֶיךָ יי אֱלֹהֵינוּ 36.
They will BOW and LIE DOWN-in-THANKS	יִכְרְעוּ וְיִפֹּלוּ. 37.
and give HONOR to Your precious NAME	וְלִכְבוֹד שִׁמְךָ יְקָר יִתֵּנוּ, 38.
and they will accept on themselves	וִיקַבְּלוּ כֻלָּם 39.
the YOKE-of-Your-EMPIRE	אֶת־עֹל מַלְכוּתֶךָ 40.
and You will quickly RULE over them for EVER and ALWAYS,	וְתִמְלֹךְ עֲלֵיהֶם מְהֵרָה לְעוֹלָם וָעֶד, 41.
BECAUSE Yours is the EMPIRE	כִּי הַמַּלְכוּת שֶׁלְּךָ הִיא 42.
and You will RULE beyond forEVER in HONOR,	וּלְעוֹלְמֵי עַד תִּמְלוֹךְ בְּכָבוֹד, 43.
As it is written in Your TORAH:	כַּכָּתוּב בְּתוֹרָתֶךָ: 44.
"ADONAI will RULE for EVER and ALWAYS" (Exodus 15.18).	יי יִמְלֹךְ לְעֹלָם וָעֶד. 45.
As it is SAID:	וְנֶאֱמַר: 46.
"ADONAI will be the RULER over the whole EARTH—	וְהָיָה יי לְמֶלֶךְ עַל כָּל־הָאָרֶץ, 47.
on that day ADONAI will be ONE	בַּיּוֹם הַהוּא יִהְיֶה יי אֶחָד 48.
and ADONAI's NAME will be ONE" (Zachariah 14.9).	וּשְׁמוֹ אֶחָד. 49.

* reconstructionist version

103

Choreography

In Temple times, people used to "dance" every word in the ending of the first paragraph of the עָלֵנוּ. When they said כּוֹרְעִים they would go down on their knees. At וּמִשְׁתַּחֲוִים they would put their hands on the ground (resting on all fours), and when they said וּמוֹדִים they would touch their heads to the floor.

Today, sometimes the rabbi and חַזָן, and sometimes the whole congregation, perform these "dance steps" during the High Holidays (once on Rosh ha-Shanah and four times on Yom Kippur).

Most of the time we just "bend our knees" during כּוֹרְעִים, "bow our head" during וּמִשְׁתַּחֲוִים, and "bow more deeply" during וּמוֹדִים.

With these actions we make God our Ruler and imagine being in God's throne room.

Practice these phrases using varieties of these words: מוֹדִים, מִשְׁתַּחֲוִים, כּוֹרְעִים.

1. וּמָרְדְּכַי לֹא יִכְרַע וְלֹא יִשְׁתַּחֲוֶה

2. בֹּאוּ נִשְׁתַּחֲוֶה וְנִכְרָעָה נִבְרְכָה לִפְנֵי יי עֹשֵׂנוּ

3. וַאֲנִי אֶשְׁתַּחֲוֶה וְאֶכְרָעָה אֲבָרְכָה לִפְנֵי יי עֹשִׂי

4. מוֹדָה אֲנִי לְפָנֶיךָ מֶלֶךְ חַי וְקַיָם שֶׁהֶחֱזַרְתָּ בִּי נִשְׁמָתִי בְּחֶמְלָה

5. מוֹדִים אֲנַחְנוּ לָךְ שָׁאַתָּה הוּא יי אֱלֹהֵינוּ וֵאלֹהֵי אֲבוֹתֵינוּ לְעוֹלָם וָעֶד

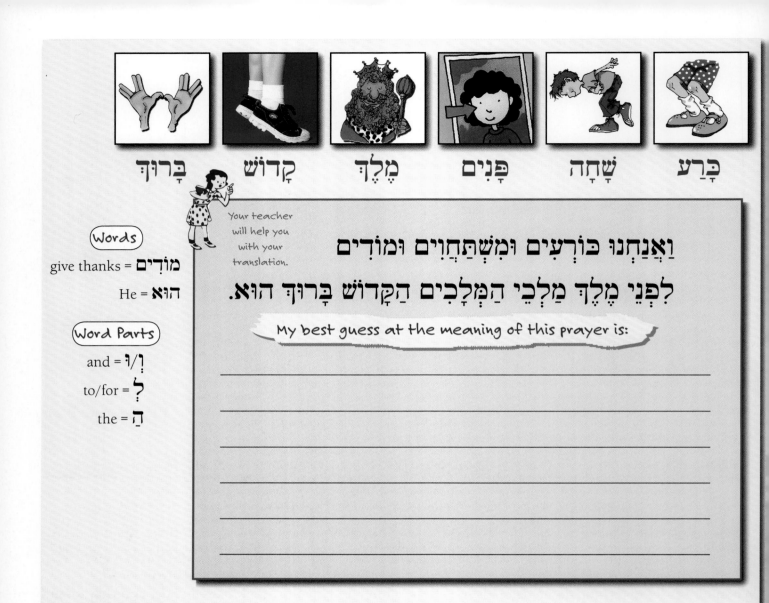

בָּרוּך קָדוֹש מֶלֶךְ פָּנִים שָׁחָה כָּרַע

Words

give thanks = מוֹדִים

He = הוּא

Word Parts

and = וְ/וּ

to/for = לְ

the = הַ

Your teacher will help you with your translation.

וַאֲנַחְנוּ כּוֹרְעִים וּמִשְׁתַּחֲוִים וּמוֹדִים
לִפְנֵי מֶלֶךְ מַלְכֵי הַמְּלָכִים הַקָדוֹש בָּרוּך הוּא.

My best guess at the meaning of this prayer is:

_____

_____

_____

_____

_____

_____

Commentary

Menasseh ben Israel lived in the 1600s. It was a time when Jews were kicked out of England. Menasseh (a Jew) wrote Oliver Cromwell (an English leader) about the עָלֵינוּ. He told Cromwell, "In our prayers we do nothing but praise God, ask for blessing, and by our worship ask for God's kindness, protection, and defense."

Questions

1. What is Menasseh ben Israel saying? What is he not saying?
2. How can you use his answer to help point your heart when you say the עָלֵינוּ?

Joshua Says עָלֵינוּ

Joshua's life was filled with close calls. He was an orphan who had no place and was then chosen by Moses to be his assistant. Joshua found a place. Joshua was chosen to lead the battle against Amalek. When Moses raised his hands inviting God's help, Joshua and the Army of Israel won. When Moses let his hands down, Israel lost. When Aaron and Hur held up Moses' hands, and they stayed in the air, with God's help, Israel was victorious.

When Israel needed spies to check out the Land of Israel, Moses changed Joshua's name. His name had been הוֹשֵׁעַ (He has saved). It became יְהוֹשֻׁעַ (God will save). Moses changed Joshua's name as a prayer, "*May God save you from misunderstanding your mission as the spies will misunderstand theirs.*" When ten of the spies chickened out on their mission, Joshua and Kalev retained faith that with God's help Israel could win.

Almost forty years later Joshua led the Families-of-Israel into the land of Canaan. He came to Jericho and found it a walled city—just about impossible to conquer. For seven days Israel marched around the city. On the seventh day they blew shofarot and shouted. With God's help, the walls came crashing down and Israel was victorious. When the battle was over, when the city was taken, Joshua told the people: עָלֵינוּ לְשַׁבֵּחַ לַאֲדוֹן הַכֹּל (It is our job to praise the MASTER-of-All).

(*Kol Bo,* Rav Hai Gaon, *Shaarei Teshuvah,* 43)

Questions
1. What reasons did Joshua have to feel obligated to praise God?
2. What are some of your reasons for feeling obligated to praise God?
3. How can knowing Joshua's connection to עָלֵינוּ help you point your heart when you say this prayer?

106

תִּקוּן עוֹלָם

Within Judaism there is a teaching known as "תִּקוּן" that is a way of life. "תִּקוּן" means to repair, heal, or restore. תִּקוּן עַצְמִי (repairing oneself), תִּקוּן קְהִלָה (repairing one's community), and תִּקוּן עוֹלָם (repairing the world) are all part of this idea of תִּקוּן.

In Pirke Avot we are taught: "Rabbi Tarfon taught: It is not up to you to complete the work (of perfecting the world), but neither are you free to quit doing it."

(Pirkei Avot, Ethics of Our Fathers, 2:16)

Questions

1. What does this teaching mean for each of us as individuals?
2. How does this quote relate to the תִּקוּן עוֹלָם work you have been doing?

Word Parts
to = לְ
in/with = בְּ

Words
Almighty = שַׁדַּי

מֶלֶךְ

עוֹלָם

תִּקֵן

Your teacher will help you with your translation.

לְתַקֵן עוֹלָם בְּמַלְכוּת שַׁדַּי

My best guess at the meaning of this prayer is:

_____

_____

_____

The תִּקּוּן עוֹלָם Story

Close your eyes (or imagine with your eyes open). Imagine everywhere in the cosmos. Imagine every when in the universe. Fill all space and all time with light. Even though we can't see God, we will think of the light as God—because God is everywhere and every when.

God decides that God wants to create the cosmos, the universe, the world, and people, but there is nowhere to do it. If God is everywhere, then anything that God created would be "toasted" by the light. Remember, no one can get too close to God. No one can see God's face and live.

So watch God do something amazing. God breathes in and leaves a hole inside of the everywhere where there is no God. Think of it as a dark room in the middle of everywhere. Inside that room God creates everything, cosmos, universe, world, and people.

But God now has a problem. God has created people in the one place where there is no God. That doesn't work at all. So imagine this. God places a bunch of empty glass light bulbs in that space. Then slowly, carefully, God begins to breathe a little light back into these containers. Imagine lots of sparks of light flying like fireflies into those light bulbs, bringing the right amount of God close to people.

Next there is an accident. Imagine the light bulbs shattering. Imagine that a jumble of sparks and broken glass tumble down together. God can do nothing about it. God can't come into the room or there will be too much God there and everything will be toasted.

God can only tell us to take a broom and start sweeping. It is our job to sweep the glass into one pile and gather the sparks of God's light into another. When all the light is gathered, everything will be great. This is called תִּקּוּן עוֹלָם, repairing the every and always. A rabbi named Isaac Luria used this story to explain our job.

(From the Lurianic Creation Myth)

Questions

1. Why does God have to leave the repair of the world up to us? What can God do to help us?
2. What things in the world would you put into the category of broken glass? What things would you categorize as sparks of God's light?
3. How does knowing this story help you know where to point your heart when you say עָלֵינוּ?

עֲצֹר!

Can you see the three letters היה in these words?

הָיָה   יִהְיֶה   לִהְיוֹת

he was = הָיָה

he will be = יִהְיֶה

to be = לִהְיוֹת

Practice these phrases and circle all the words that contain the root היה.

1. וְהוּא הָיָה וְהוּא הֹוֶה וְהוּא יִהְיֶה

2. לִהְיוֹת מוֹשְׁלִים בְּקֶרֶב תֵּבֵל

3. בָּרוּךְ שֶׁאָמַר וְהָיָה הָעוֹלָם בָּרוּךְ הוּא

4. בַּיּוֹם הַהוּא יִהְיֶה יי אֶחָד

5. וְהָיוּ הַדְּבָרִים הָאֵלֶּה אֲשֶׁר אָנֹכִי מְצַוְּךָ הַיּוֹם עַל־לְבָבֶךָ

Word Parts

in/with = בְּ

and = וְ/וּ

his = וֹ■

Words

that = הַהוּא

He will be = יִהְיֶה

name = שֵׁם

יוֹם

1

אֶחָד

Your teacher will help you with your translation.

בַּיּוֹם הַהוּא יִהְיֶה יי אֶחָד וּשְׁמוֹ אֶחָד

My best guess at the meaning of this prayer is:

_____

_____

_____

110

The Jewel

This jewel was the biggest and the best of all the jewels that came out of the mine. The king wanted it from the minute he saw it. It was the best. He had to have it. He said, "If it is the best, if it is the biggest, it is mine!"

The king had first seen the jewel when he was visiting his ruby mine. He saw it lying in a wagon of unpolished stones. He picked it up, put it in his pocket, said, "Mine," and walked out of the mine. He knew it was the biggest and the best. The king didn't need to see anything else.

The king gave the giant ruby to the royal jeweler. He said to him, "Polish it. Make it perfect." The jeweler put the ocular, magnifying glass, in his eye. He looked at every side of the ruby. He looked over and over again. Finally, in a soft and shaky voice, he said, "Your majesty, there is a crack in this stone."

The king said, "So fix it."

The jeweler said, "I am sorry, your majesty, but it cannot be done."

The king went and got another royal jeweler. This one put in his ocular. This one also looked and looked. After a long time this one said, "Your majesty, the best thing we can do is cut the big stone into three beautiful smaller stones. Each one of the three will be wonderful."

The king said, "Then it will not be the biggest or the best." Then the king went and got another new royal jeweler. The king got a lot of new royal jewelers because not one of them knew how to fix a crack in a large and beautiful ruby.

The king left the ruby on the table. One day a visitor came to the palace. He said, "Your majesty, may I look at your stone?" The king gave permission. The visitor took out his ocular and looked and looked. After a long time he said, "I can make your stone into something beautiful."

The king asked, "Will it be big? Will it be beautiful? Will it be perfect?"

The visitor said, "Yes. Yes. Yes." He took the stone and went into the workshop. Everywhere in the palace you could hear the grinding and the polishing. It took three days.

The visitor came before the king with the jewel under a black cloth. The king asked, "Is it still big?" The visitor nodded. "Is it still beautiful?" The visitor nodded. "Is it perfect?" The visitor nodded. Then the king asked, "How did you get rid of the crack?"

The visitor said, "The crack is still here, your majesty."

The king started to say, "But, but, but, but..." when the visitor pulled the cloth off the ruby. Everyone in the palace gasped. The stone was huge. It was beautiful. And at the center of the stone was now carved a wonderful rose. The crack had become the stem.

The king opened his mouth and said, "Wow." Then the king did something unusual. He stopped talking. He just looked and looked at the jewel. Later he rewarded the jeweler. He showed everyone who came to the palace his jewel with a rose. At the end of the story the king told everyone, "I learned the most important lesson of my life that day."

Things in the kingdom were much better from that day on. (A story of the Maggid of Dubnow)

Questions

1. What do you think the rose in the ruby taught the king?
2. How is this story a story about תִּקּוּן עוֹלָם?
3. How can knowing this story help you point your heart when you say the עָלֵינוּ?

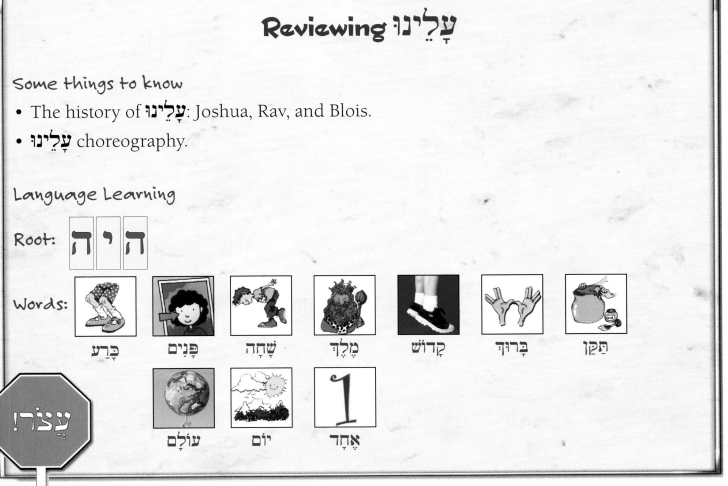

Reviewing עָלֵינוּ

Some things to know

- The history of עָלֵינוּ: Joshua, Rav, and Blois.
- עָלֵינוּ choreography.

Language Learning

Root: ה י ה

Words: כָּרַע   פָּנִים   שָׁחָה   מֶלֶךְ   קָדוֹשׁ   בָּרוּךְ   תִּקֵּן

עוֹלָם   יוֹם   אֶחָד

עֲצֹר!

קַדִּישׁ

When the Babylonians destroyed Jerusalem and carried away all the survivors as prisoners, the Jews started *yeshivot* (Torah schools) in Babylonia. Later, when Ezra and Neḥemiah organized the return to the Land of Israel, they started new yeshivot. No matter what difficulties they faced, no matter how sad they were, Jews gathered to study the Torah and fit it into their lives. The קַדִּישׁ started out as a prayer said at the end of study sessions. It said "God is great" and "we can find the strength to go on" (*Sotah* 49a).

The קַדִּישׁ is said seven times a day because of Psalm 119.164, "SEVEN TIMES A DAY I WILL PRAISE YOU." There are five kinds of קַדִּישִׁים: (1) חֲצִי קַדִּישׁ, which divides one part of a service from another; (2) קַדִּישׁ שָׁלֵם, which is said at the end of the עֲמִידָה; (3) קַדִּישׁ יָתוֹם, which is the mourner's קַדִּישׁ; (4) קַדִּישׁ דְּרַבָּנָן, the rabbis' קַדִּישׁ, which is said at the end of a study session; (5) קַדִּישׁ לְאִתְחַדְתָּא, which is said after a burial or finishing a book of the Talmud.

Even though קַדִּישׁ is said for many other purposes, it became most famous as a prayer said by mourners. Rabbi Isaac Luria taught, "When קַדִּישׁ יָתוֹם is said for eleven months by mourners, it helps to move a soul from *Gehinom* (purgatory) to *Gan Eden* (paradise). When קַדִּישׁ is said on a *Yahrtzeit* it helps to lift a soul to higher levels of paradise."

Question: How can the קַדִּישׁ move a soul to *Gan Eden*? How can it lift a soul to higher levels?

The קַדִּישׁ is made up of ten expressions of praise. It is also a prayer that takes a minyan, a community of ten. In the *Zohar* we are taught (Aḥarei Mot), "The person for whom קַדִּישׁ is being said gets credit for gathering ten Jews." We are also told there, "The words of the קַדִּישׁ make God feel better."

Question: How can the words of the קַדִּישׁ make God feel better?

In this unit you will learn:
- The many uses of the קַדִּישׁ
- The purpose of the mourner's קַדִּישׁ.

Let God's Great NAME be (1) BIG and (2) HOLY	יִתְגַּדַּל וְיִתְקַדַּשׁ שְׁמֵהּ רַבָּא .1
in this world that God CREATED with will.	בְּעָלְמָא דִּי בְרָא כִרְעוּתֵהּ .2
Let God completely RULE the EMPIRE	וְיַמְלִיךְ מַלְכוּתֵהּ .3
in this life and in these days,	בְּחַיֵּיכוֹן וּבְיוֹמֵיכוֹן .4
and in the lifetime of all the Families-of-Israel.	וּבְחַיֵּי דְכָל-בֵּית יִשְׂרָאֵל .5
Let this happen QUICKLY in a nearby time	בַּעֲגָלָה וּבִזְמַן קָרִיב .6
and let us say: "AMEN."	וְאִמְרוּ אָמֵן. .7
Let God's Great NAME be blessed	יְהֵא שְׁמֵהּ רַבָּא מְבָרַךְ .8
in the world and in the world of worlds—FOREVER.	לְעָלַם וּלְעָלְמֵי עָלְמַיָּא. .9
(3) Blessed, (4) Called AMAZING, (5) Glorified	יִתְבָּרַךְ וְיִשְׁתַּבַּח וְיִתְפָּאַר .10
(6) Extolled, (7) Honored, (8) Respected,	וְיִתְרוֹמַם וְיִתְנַשֵּׂא וְיִתְהַדָּר .11
(9) Lifted Up and (10) HALLELUYAHed	וְיִתְעַלֶּה וְיִתְהַלָּל .12
be the NAME of the Holy-ONE-Who-is-to-be-Blessed	שְׁמֵהּ דְּקֻדְשָׁא בְּרִיךְ הוּא .13
above anything we can Bless and Sing	לְעֵלָּא מִן כָּל-בִּרְכָתָא וְשִׁירָתָא .14
above all prayers and consolations	תֻּשְׁבְּחָתָא וְנֶחֱמָתָא .15
that we can say in this world.	דַּאֲמִירָן בְּעָלְמָא .16
And let us say, "AMEN."	וְאִמְרוּ אָמֵן. .17
Let there be a great PEACE from heaven.	יְהֵא שְׁלָמָא רַבָּא מִן שְׁמַיָּא .18
Let us have a good life—and the same for all of Israel	וְחַיִּים עָלֵינוּ וְעַל כָּל-יִשְׂרָאֵל .19
and let us say: "Amen."	וְאִמְרוּ אָמֵן. .20
May the One-Who-Makes PEACE in the heavens above	עוֹשֶׂה שָׁלוֹם בִּמְרוֹמָיו .21
May that One make PEACE for us	הוּא יַעֲשֶׂה שָׁלוֹם עָלֵינוּ .22
and for all of Israel	וְעַל כָּל-יִשְׂרָאֵל .23
and let us say: "AMEN."	וְאִמְרוּ אָמֵן. .24

Meet Aramaic

Aramaic is a language that is connected to Arabic, Hebrew, Ethiopic, and Akkadian (ancient Babylonian and Assyrian). It is particularly closely related to Hebrew, and was written in a variety of alphabetic scripts. What we call "Hebrew" writing is actually an Aramaic script.

Aramaic is a really old language that comes from almost three thousand years ago (900-700 B.C.E.). Aramaic was used by the conquering Assyrians as a language of administrative communication, and following them by the Babylonian and Persian empires, which ruled from India to Ethiopia, and employed Aramaic as the official language. Portions of the Bible, parts of Ezra and Daniel, are in Aramaic. Parts of the Talmud, the midrash, and other important books are also in Aramaic. So is the קַדִּיש.

גָּדוֹל	חַיֵּיכוֹן
קָדוֹש	שְׁמֵהּ
מֶלֶךְ	שִׁירָתָא
חַי	בִּרְכָתָא
יוֹם	מַלְכוּתֵהּ
שֵׁם	יִתְגַּדַּל
הָעוֹלָם	יוֹמֵיכוֹן
שִׁיר	עָלְמָא
בְּרָכָה	יִתְקַדַּש

Your teacher will help you with your translation.

Words

name = שֵׁם
great = רַבָּה

קָדוֹש

גָּדוֹל

יִתְגַּדַּל וְיִתְקַדַּש שְׁמֵהּ רַבָּא

My best guess at the meaning of this prayer is:

_____

_____

_____

Dream קַדִּישׁ

An old woman is in her bedroom in Prague. The angel of death enters and gets ready to take her. She says, "Not yet." He says, "What's wrong?" She says, "I was the maid for the rabbi, and the community takes good care of me, but I need someone to say קַדִּישׁ for me." The angel asked, "Do you have a relative?" The woman answered, "I have a great-grandson whom I have never met. He lives in Germany." "That can be arranged," said the angel.

That night the woman died. The people of Prague found her with a big smile on her face. That night Joseph, her great-grandson, had a dream. In that dream an old woman in white appeared. She put his face in her hands and said, "I am your great-grandmother. Say קַדִּישׁ for me. There is no one else to do it but you."

Joseph woke in the morning. He barely remembered the old woman who lived in Prague. He had nothing to do with his family anymore. He had nothing to do with the Jewish people either. He went to his dresser and took out his bar mitzvah *tallit*. He had not thought about it in years. He took it and started to walk.

He walked and walked through the city, through the forest, past fields, not knowing where he was going, but knowing where he should go. He came to a small Jewish village and made his way to the synagogue. He told his story to the *shamash*, the spiritual custodian of the shul. The *shamash* taught him the words of the קַדִּישׁ. He said it every day for eleven months.

קַדִּישׁ Rules

1. קַדִּישׁ takes a מִנְיָן.
2. A mourner recites קַדִּישׁ for eleven months minus one day.
3. קַדִּישׁ is said on the *Yahrtzeit*, the anniversary of the death.
3. קַדִּישׁ is not said before the funeral.
4. Traditionally, one says קַדִּישׁ for relatives: husband/wife, brother. sister, mother, father, child—and for one's teacher.
5. Adoptive children have the same obligations as natural children to say קַדִּישׁ.
6. There is a custom that is frowned upon: hiring another person to say קַדִּישׁ for you if you cannot get to synagogue.

When the year was over many things had changed. Joseph had sold his apartment in the city and moved to this village. He became part of the community. He met a woman, and they were ready to get married. In saying קַדִּישׁ Joseph found his way back to his people.

(Based on "Amen" in *Ze Zidovskeho Ghetta* by A. Hoffman and R. Heuerova, found in *Jewish Tales from Eastern Europe*, Nadia Grosser Nagarajan)

Questions

1. What did the קַדִּישׁ do for the great grandmother? What did it do for Joseph?
2. What does this story teach about saying the mourner's קַדִּישׁ?
3. How can remembering this story help you know where to point your heart when you participate in the mourner's קַדִּישׁ?

עֲצֹר!

117

Kaddish de-Rabbanan

Practice the Kaddish de-Rabbanan.

1. יִתְגַּדַּל וְיִתְקַדַּשׁ שְׁמֵהּ רַבָּא בְּעָלְמָא דִּי בְרָא כִרְעוּתֵהּ וְיַמְלִיךְ מַלְכוּתֵהּ

2. בְּחַיֵּיכוֹן וּבְיוֹמֵיכוֹן וּבְחַיֵּי דְכָל־בֵּית יִשְׂרָאֵל בַּעֲגָלָה וּבִזְמַן קָרִיב וְאִמְרוּ אָמֵן

3. יְהֵא שְׁמֵהּ רַבָּא מְבָרַךְ לְעָלַם וּלְעָלְמֵי עָלְמַיָּא

4. יִתְבָּרַךְ וְיִשְׁתַּבַּח וְיִתְפָּאַר וְיִתְרוֹמַם וְיִתְנַשֵּׂא וְיִתְהַדָּר וְיִתְעַלֶּה

5. וְיִתְהַלָּל שְׁמֵהּ דְּקֻדְשָׁא בְּרִיךְ הוּא לְעֵלָּא מִן כָּל־בִּרְכָתָא וְשִׁירָתָא

6. תֻּשְׁבְּחָתָא וְנֶחֱמָתָא דַּאֲמִירָן בְּעָלְמָא וְאִמְרוּ אָמֵן

7. עַל יִשְׂרָאֵל וְעַל רַבָּנָן וְעַל תַּלְמִידֵיהוֹן וְעַל כָּל־תַּלְמִידֵי תַלְמִידֵיהוֹן

8. וְעַל כָּל־מָאן דְּעָסְקִין בְּאוֹרַיְתָא דִּי בְאַתְרָא הָדֵין

9. וְדִי בְּכָל־אֲתַר וַאֲתַר יְהֵא לְהוֹן וּלְכוֹן שְׁלָמָא רַבָּא

10. חִנָּא וְחִסְדָּא וְרַחֲמִין וְחַיִּין אֲרִיכִין וּמְזוֹנָא רְוִיחָא

11. וּפוּרְקָנָא מִן קֳדָם אֲבוּהוֹן דִּי בִשְׁמַיָּה וְאִמְרוּ אָמֵן

12. יְהֵא שְׁלָמָא רַבָּא מִן שְׁמַיָּא וְחַיִּים עָלֵינוּ וְעַל כָּל־יִשְׂרָאֵל וְאִמְרוּ אָמֵן.

13. עוֹשֶׂה שָׁלוֹם בִּמְרוֹמָיו הוּא יַעֲשֶׂה שָׁלוֹם עָלֵינוּ וְעַל כָּל־יִשְׂרָאֵל וְאִמְרוּ אָמֵן.

עָשָׂה שָׁלוֹם עַל יִשְׂרָאֵל אָמַר אָמֵן

Words

heavens = מָרוֹם

he = הוּא

Word Parts

in/with = בְּ

and = וְ/וּ

our = ■נוּ

his = ■יו

Your teacher will help you with your translation.

עוֹשֶׂה שָׁלוֹם בִּמְרוֹמָיו הוּא יַעֲשֶׂה שָׁלוֹם עָלֵינוּ
וְעַל כָּל-יִשְׂרָאֵל וְאִמְרוּ אָמֵן.

My best guess at the meaning of this prayer is:

_____

_____

_____

Comment

The midrash teaches this about peace:

שָׁלוֹם is a precious thing. For all the good deeds and ethical actions that Abraham did the only reward given to him was שָׁלוֹם. The Torah says, "BUT YOU SHALL GO TO YOUR FATHERS IN שָׁלוֹם" (Genesis 15.15). Likewise in the case of our father Jacob, you find that he asked for שָׁלוֹם from God; for it says, "SO THAT I COME BACK TO MY FATHER'S HOUSE IN שָׁלוֹם..." (Genesis 28.21). In the case of Aaron, you also find that he was praised by God for nothing so much as שָׁלוֹם; for it says, "MY COVENANT WITH HIM WAS OF LIFE AND שָׁלוֹם..." (Malachi 2.5). You will also find that the Torah was compared above all to שָׁלוֹם; as it says, "ALL HER PATHS ARE שָׁלוֹם" (Proverbs 3.17). Thus also you find that the Holy One comforts Jerusalem above all with the promise of שָׁלוֹם; for it says, "AND MY PEOPLE SHALL LIVE IN שָׁלוֹם" (Isaiah 32.18). Israel is blessed every day with שָׁלוֹם; for it says, "AND GIVES YOU שָׁלוֹם" (Num. 6.26).

(*Midrash Rabbah, Numbers 11.7*)

Questions

1. Why does the קַדִּישׁ end with describing God as a peace-maker?
2. What does that do for the person saying קַדִּישׁ? What does it do for the person about whom קַדִּישׁ is being said?
3. How can thinking about God as a peacemaker help you say or respond to קַדִּישׁ?

Rabbi Akiva was walking through a cemetery. He saw a naked man, covered in soot, carrying a huge bundle of wood on his head. The man was running with the load. He was shouting the Aramaic version of "I'm late. I'm late. If I don't finish they will make it worse." Rabbi Akiva asked the man, "Is there anything I can do to help? If you are poor, can I buy you out of this debt to these masters who are way too demanding?" The man said, "You are talking to a dead man. I am in *Gehinom*, the place one waits before going on to the Garden of Eden. I will be here forever. Every night they boil me in oil using the wood I collect."

Rabbi Akiva asked, "What is your name?" The man answered, "Akiva." The rabbi asked further, "What was your crime? What will help you to move on?" The man answered, "I was a tax collector, and I took bribes from the rich and taxed the poor to death to make it up. They told me that my only way out of *Gehinom* was for a child of mine to say the קָדִישׁ. I need that child to count as one of my good deeds." In those days one said the קָדִישׁ only at the end of Torah study. It was not a mourner's prayer. The person with the best Torah insight led it.

Rabbi Akiva left Akiva and went looking for a child. He found a son. The son was living as a non-Jew. He did not know even one Hebrew letter. The Jewish community had abandoned him. Rabbi Akiva began to teach him, but the son's heart was not in his studies. Rabbi Akiva tried all his best teacher tricks—nothing worked.

Rabbi Akiva prayed to God and asked for the child's heart to be opened. Slowly the lessons went better. Once, when Rabbi Akiva brought the son to a Torah study, the son was picked to lead the קַדִּישׁ. When the prayer was over, Akiva went to the Garden of Eden.

That night Rabbi Akiva had a dream. In the dream he heard Akiva's voice. "You saved me from *Gehinom*. May your soul go quickly to the Garden of Eden in its time." In his dream, Rabbi Akiva said, "Eternal, Your NAME lasts forever, Your memory is for all generations" (Ps 102.13). This is when the mourner's קַדִּישׁ began (*Mahzor Vitry*).

Questions

1. According to this story, what does קַדִּישׁ do for the dead person?
2. According to this story, what does קַדִּישׁ do for the person who says it?
3. How can remembering this story help you know where to point your heart when you participate in the mourner's קַדִּישׁ?

The קַדִּישׁ שָׁלֵם

The קַדִּישׁ שָׁלֵם is said at the end of the עֲמִידָה. It is made up of most of the קַדִּישׁ יָתוֹם (mourner's קַדִּישׁ) but adds this phrase.

Practice this phrase from the קַדִּישׁ שָׁלֵם.

1. תִּתְקַבֵּל צְלוֹתְהוֹן וּבָעוּתְהוֹן

2. דְּכָל יִשְׂרָאֵל

3. קֳדָם אֲבוּהוֹן דִי בִשְׁמַיָּא וְאִמְרוּ אָמֵן.

Reviewing the Kaddish

Some things to know

- קַדִּישׁ started as a study prayer.
- There are five different kinds of קַדִּישִׁים.
- חֲצִי קַדִּישׁ divides parts of the service.
- קַדִּישׁ יָתוֹם is a way of becoming a "good deed" for a person who has passed away.

Language Learning

Words:

 גָּדוֹל
 קָדוֹשׁ
 עָשָׂה
 שָׁלוֹם
 עַל
 יִשְׂרָאֵל
 אָמַר

 אָמֵן

Famous Quote: קַדִּישׁ is the source of:

עוֹשֶׂה שָׁלוֹם בִּמְרוֹמָיו הוּא יַעֲשֶׂה שָׁלוֹם עָלֵינוּ
וְעַל כָּל־יִשְׂרָאֵל וְאִמְרוּ אָמֵן.

 עֲצֹר!

122

אֲדוֹן עוֹלָם

אֲדוֹן עוֹלָם is a song that is sometimes sung at the beginning of services, that is sung at the end of services, and that is sung at Moroccan Jewish weddings. It is a song that talks about God.

There are a number of midrashim that tell the story of Abraham discovering that there was only one God by looking at nature and by thinking about the world. In the Talmud we are told that Abraham was the first one to call God אֲדוֹן (master) (*Brakhot* 7b/Genesis 15.8). When we sing אֲדוֹן עוֹלָם we are like Abraham, discovering God in the world, God in our experience, and figuring out things about God through thinking. In the same Talmudic passage we are also told that Daniel's prayers were answered only because of his connection as a descendent of Abraham. We, too, come from Abraham.

It is unsure who wrote אֲדוֹן עוֹלָם. Various opinions include: Rabban Yohanan ben Zakkai, Rabbi Sherira Gaon or his son Rabbi Hai Gaon, or Solomon Ibn Gabirol. Our best guess, however, is that it started out as an evening prayer. The last verse that talks about going to sleep and waking up safely—because God is with us—gives it away.

In this unit you will learn:
- The story of אֲדוֹן עוֹלָם.
- Some Jewish Ideas about God.

123

אֲדוֹן עוֹלָם

MASTER of the Cosmos who RULED	אֲדוֹן עוֹלָם אֲשֶׁר מָלַךְ	1.
Before any LIFE was CREATED	בְּטֶרֶם כָּל־יְצִיר נִבְרָא	2.
At the time when all was MADE by God's WILL	לְעֵת נַעֲשָׂה בְחֶפְצוֹ כֹּל	3.
Then was God's name called RULER.	אֲזַי מֶלֶךְ שְׁמוֹ נִקְרָא.	4.
After everything is OVER	וְאַחֲרֵי כִּכְלוֹת הַכֹּל	5.
ALONE—the AWESOME-One will RULE	לְבַדּוֹ יִמְלֹךְ נוֹרָא	6.
God WAS—God IS—	וְהוּא הָיָה וְהוּא הֹוֶה	7.
and God WILL BE in glory.	וְהוּא יִהְיֶה בְּתִפְאָרָה.	8.
God is the ONE—there is no SECOND	וְהוּא אֶחָד וְאֵין שֵׁנִי	9.
That can COMPARE to GOD—or be BESIDE God	לְהַמְשִׁיל לוֹ לְהַחְבִּירָה	10.
God has no BEGINNING—God has no END	בְּלִי רֵאשִׁית בְּלִי תַכְלִית	11.
POWER and DOMINION belong to GOD.	וְלוֹ הָעֹז וְהַמִּשְׂרָה.	12.
God is MY GOD—and MY LIVING REDEEMER	וְהוּא אֵלִי וְחַי גֹּאֲלִי	13.
The ROCK of My fate—in the TIME of NEED	וְצוּר חֶבְלִי בְּעֵת צָרָה	14.
God is my FLAG and my REFUGE	וְהוּא נִסִּי וּמָנוֹס לִי	15.
God is the PORTION of my CUP on the day I CALL.	מְנָת כּוֹסִי בְּיוֹם אֶקְרָא.	16.
Into God's hand I will trust my spirit	בְּיָדוֹ אַפְקִיד רוּחִי	17.
Both when I sleep and when I am awake	בְּעֵת אִישָׁן וְאָעִירָה	18.
And with my spirit and with my body	וְעִם רוּחִי גְוִיָּתִי	19.
ADONAI is with me and I will not be afraid.	יְיָ לִי וְלֹא אִירָא.	20.

Commentary: אֲדוֹן עוֹלָם probably started out as a nighttime prayer. Here is a midrash that connects to the prayer.

In this world, when you put money in a bank, your bills lose their identity. One is exchanged for the next. But the Holy One is different. God takes old, worn-out souls that have been used all day and returns them each morning as new. Souls that were worn out are made new after a night of sleep (Sokher Tov, Psalm 25.2).

Questions: (1) Which lines in the prayer are connected to this image? (2) How can knowing this midrash help you point your heart when you sing אֲדוֹן עוֹלָם?

Talk About God

Maimonides taught that there were thirteen things that every Jew was supposed to believe. He was an important teacher who lived in the 1200s. Underline the places where you agree with him.

1. God is perfect and created all that exists.
2. Nothing is the same as God.
3. God is not physical and isn't affected by physical things.
4. God was and is forever.
5. We have to worship God and nothing else.
6. God communicates with people through prophecy.
7. Moses is the most important prophet.
8. The Torah came from God.
9. The Torah can't be changed.
10. God cares and God is everywhere.
11. God rewards and punishes people.
12. God will send a Messiah or messianic era.
13. God will put our souls back in our bodies and let us live again.

(Commentary on the Mishnah Sanhedrin, chap. 10),

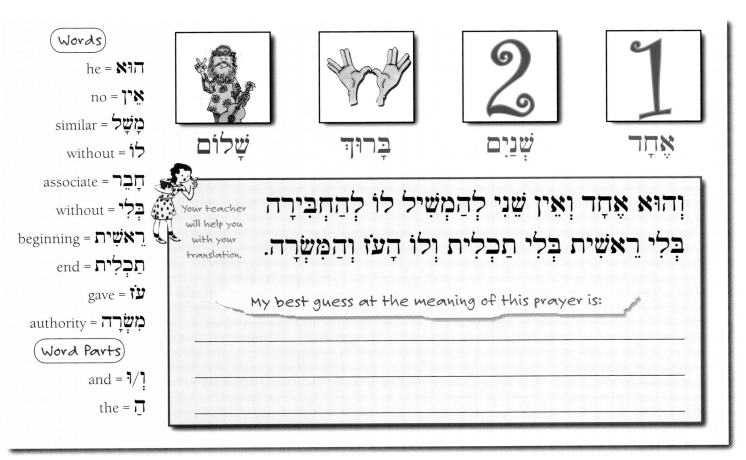

Words

he = הוּא

no = אֵין

similar = מָשָׁל

without = לוֹ

associate = חָבֵר

without = בְּלִי

beginning = רֵאשִׁית

end = תַכְלִית

gave = עֹז

authority = מִשְׂרָה

Word Parts

and = וְ / וּ

the = הַ

שָׁלוֹם   בָּרוּךְ   שְׁנַיִם   אֶחָד

וְהוּא אֶחָד וְאֵין שֵׁנִי לְהַמְשִׁיל לוֹ לְהַחְבִּירָה
בְּלִי רֵאשִׁית בְּלִי תַכְלִית וְלוֹ הָעֹז וְהַמִּשְׂרָה.

Your teacher will help you with your translation.

My best guess at the meaning of this prayer is:

_____

_____

_____

The Great Garden

A ruler planted an amazing garden. In the middle of the garden the ruler had an amazing maze built. Each visitor received a letter from the ruler that said, "Enter by the door of the maze and seek the center. There you will find what you have been seeking your whole life."

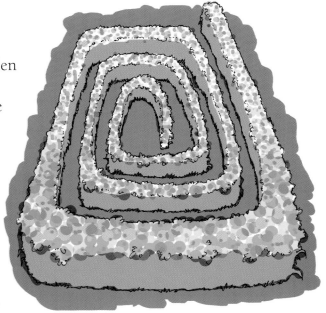

Many entered and became lost. They found the maze too hard, and they discovered enough beautiful places along the way that they gave up. Most people just enjoyed the hedge, the benches, and the flowers. They gave up their quest. Many of them cried out, "This is too hard. Why did you hide our heart's desire in the center of a difficult maze?"

Then they heard the ruler call out from the center. "It is only by seeking and wandering that you can be prepared to find me. The seeking is a necessary part of the finding." Then they realized that finding the ruler, being close to the ruler, was the thing they desired most.

(Kabbalistic parable drawn from *Chassidic Stories Retold*, edited by Edith Samuel)

עֲצֹר!

Questions

1. If the Ruler in this story is God, explain the other symbols.
2. What is the lesson of this story?
3. How can knowing this story help you to point your heart when you say אֲדוֹן עוֹלָם?

הַבְדָּלָה

Havdalah is a way of ending Shabbat. It is a ceremony that uses a candle, a cup of wine, and a spice box. In a sense, we end Shabbat in the same ways we begin it.

Introduction: First we say a collection of verses from five different places in the Torah. These verses talk about "cup" and "light." They describe the symbols that will be used in this service. These verses also talk about the time in the future when God will help us fix and perfect the world. The end of Shabbat is a time when we hope for the best possible future.

Wine: Wine is used to welcome Shabbat. The blessing over wine is also used to organize the ending of Shabbat. Every time we use wine it is a celebration. It is traditional to fill the cup to overflowing and spill a little bit as we lift it (*Eruvim* 65a). The Rama said, "The wine shows that we are blessed" (Ch. 291, 1).

Spice: There is a tradition that on Shabbat we are given a נְשָׁמָה יְתֵרָה, an extra soul. We smell spices at the end of Shabbat to give us a boost when that extra soul is taken from us. Their smell refreshes us (Abudarham).

Fire: In the Torah we are told that one should not create fire on Shabbat. In the Talmud (*Pesaḥim* 53b) we are taught that God showed Adam and Eve how to create fire after the first Shabbat was over. God gave them fire as a tool. At the end of Shabbat we celebrate that gift by creating fire and saying a blessing over it.

הַבְדָּלָה: The last blessing in the service is a blessing over distinctions. The midrash teaches that Adam and Eve learned about distinctions during the first הַבְדָּלָה. They saw shadow and light, and they saw the difference between holy and ordinary. We use the end of Shabbat to learn this same lesson.

In this unit you will learn:

• The הַבְדָּלָה service.

• The root בדל

127

הַבְדָּלָה

English	#	Hebrew
Here is God—my SALVATION.	1.	הִנֵּה אֵל יְשׁוּעָתִי
I will TRUST and not BE AFRAID.	2.	אֶבְטַח וְלֹא אֶפְחָד.
ADONAI is my STRENGTH and MY GOD-SONG	3.	כִּי עָזִּי וְזִמְרָת יָהּ יי
and will be my SALVATION.	4.	וַיְהִי לִי לִישׁוּעָה.
You can draw water in JOY	5.	וּשְׁאַבְתֶּם מַיִם בְּשָׂשׂוֹן
from the WELLSPRINGS of SALVATION. (Isaiah 12.2-3)	6.	מִמַּעַיְנֵי הַיְשׁוּעָה.
Salvation is ADONAI's	7.	לַיי הַיְשׁוּעָה
for Your PEOPLE whom you BLESSED. Selah. (Psalm 3.9)	8.	עַל עַמְּךָ בִרְכָתֶךָ סֶּלָה.
ADONAI of Hosts is WITH US—	9.	יי צְבָאוֹת עִמָּנוּ
the God of Jacob is our FORTRESS. Selah. (Psalm 46.12)	10.	מִשְׂגָּב לָנוּ אֱלֹהֵי יַעֲקֹב סֶלָה.
ADONAI of Hosts	11.	יי צְבָאוֹת
HAPPY are people who TRUST in You.	12.	אַשְׁרֵי אָדָם בֹּטֵחַ בָּךְ.
ADONAI saves	13.	יי הוֹשִׁיעָה
THE RULER Who will ANSWER us on the day that we CALL. (Psalm 84.13)	14.	הַמֶּלֶךְ יַעֲנֵנוּ בְיוֹם קָרְאֵנוּ.
For the Jews there was LIGHT	15.	לַיְּהוּדִים הָיְתָה אוֹרָה
and GLADNESS and JOY and HONOR (Esther 8.16)	16.	וְשִׂמְחָה וְשָׂשׂוֹן וִיקָר.
so may there be for US.	17.	כֵּן תִּהְיֶה לָנוּ.
I lift up the cup of SALVATION	18.	כּוֹס יְשׁוּעוֹת אֶשָּׂא
And will call on ADONAI's NAME. (Psalm 116.13)	19.	וּבְשֵׁם יי אֶקְרָא.
Praised are You ADONAI	20.	בָּרוּךְ אַתָּה יי
our God Ruler of the Cosmos	21.	אֱלֹהֵינוּ מֶלֶךְ הָעוֹלָם
the CREATOR-of-FRUIT-of-the-VINE.	22.	בּוֹרֵא פְּרִי הַגָּפֶן.

Praised are You ADONAI	בָּרוּךְ אַתָּה יי 23.
our God Ruler of the Cosmos	אֱלֹהֵינוּ מֶלֶךְ הָעוֹלָם 24.
the CREATOR-of-kinds-of-SPICES.	בּוֹרֵא מִינֵי בְשָׂמִים. 25.
Praised are You ADONAI	בָּרוּךְ אַתָּה יי 26.
our God Ruler of the Cosmos	אֱלֹהֵינוּ מֶלֶךְ הָעוֹלָם 27.
the CREATOR-of-the LIGHTS-of-FIRE.	בּוֹרֵא מְאוֹרֵי הָאֵשׁ. 28.
Praised are You ADONAI	בָּרוּךְ אַתָּה יי 29.
our God Ruler of the Cosmos	אֱלֹהֵינוּ מֶלֶךְ הָעוֹלָם 30.
the ONE-Who-DIVIDES between HOLY and ORDINARY	הַמַּבְדִיל בֵּין קֹדֶשׁ לְחוֹל 31.
between LIGHT and DARKNESS	בֵּין אוֹר לְחֹשֶׁךְ 32.
between ISRAEL and OTHER NATIONS	בֵּין יִשְׂרָאֵל לָעַמִּים 33.
between the SEVENTH DAY	בֵּין יוֹם הַשְּׁבִיעִי 34.
and the SIX DAYS of CREATION	לְשֵׁשֶׁת יְמֵי הַמַּעֲשֶׂה. 35.
Praised are You ADONAI	בָּרוּךְ אַתָּה יי 36.
the ONE-Who-DIVIDES between HOLY and ORDINARY.	הַמַּבְדִיל בֵּין קֹדֶשׁ לְחוֹל. 37.

Commentary

It is a custom to have a third meal near the end of Shabbat. After Shabbat, it was a tradition to bring in spices and heat them like incense on the fire. These spices help people to keep some of the lessons of Shabbat with them once the week has begun. This custom grew into the הַבְדָּלָה service (Saadia).

Question: What things can a person take from Shabbat into the week?

הַבְדָּלָה Choreography

1. הַבְדָּלָה can be made on Saturday night after three stars are in the sky. In synagogue, it is said after the end of the evening service.

2. הַבְדָּלָה is usually done standing. The leader picks up the Kiddush cup in his or her right hand and spills a little wine. Often the spices are in the left hand.

3. Usually a different person is holding the candle. Sometimes it is sitting in a candle holder.

4. The opening paragraph and the בְּרָכָה over the wine are said. The wine is put down. It is not sipped at this point.

5. The spices are taken in the right hand and the בְּרָכָה over the spices is said. Then the spice box is put down.

6. The בְּרָכָה over fire is now said. A הַבְדָּלָה candle must have at least two wicks. This makes it a torch. Everyone takes his or her hand, curls his or her fingers and looks at the shadow of the fingers across the palm. They also look at the reflection of fire in the fingernails.

7. The wine cup is picked up again and the final בְּרָכָה, the one that celebrates divisions, is said. At the end of this בְּרָכָה someone drinks the wine. It is then traditional to put out the candle in some of the wine.

8. It is also traditional to hug and sway during the songs that follow.

 בָּרוּךְ  אַתָּה  מֶלֶךְ  עוֹלָם  פְּרִי הַגָּפֶן  בְּשָׂמִים

 אוֹר

 אֵשׁ

(Words)

בּוֹרֵא = create

מִינֵי = kinds of

(Word Parts)

הַ = the

בָּרוּךְ אַתָּה יי אֱלֹהֵינוּ מֶלֶךְ הָעוֹלָם בּוֹרֵא פְּרִי הַגָּפֶן.

בָּרוּךְ אַתָּה יי אֱלֹהֵינוּ מֶלֶךְ הָעוֹלָם בּוֹרֵא מִינֵי בְשָׂמִים.

בָּרוּךְ אַתָּה יי אֱלֹהֵינוּ מֶלֶךְ הָעוֹלָם בּוֹרֵא מְאוֹרֵי הָאֵשׁ.

My best guess at the meaning of this prayer is:

_____

_____

_____

_____

_____

Commentary

The concluding moments of Shabbat are a time of uncertainty. When the holiness of Shabbat fades we again begin to worry about what is to come. With the departure of the Holy Shabbat and the beginning of the work week it is important to make a distinction between the holy and the ordinary *(ArtScroll Siddur)*.

Questions

1. How does one tell the difference between holy and ordinary?
2. Why is the beginning of the week an important time to make this distinction?

Adam and Eve

Adam and Eve spent their first Shabbat in the Garden of Eden. They knew that when the day was over, when night came, they would have to leave the garden. As it began to get dark they got scared. The darker it got, the more their fear grew. Adam was scared that the serpent would return and bite him in the heel. God told Adam to pick up two rocks. One rock was darkness. The other was the shadow of death. Adam banged the two rocks together, and out came a spark. The spark lit a fire, the fire lit a torch, and the torch was held high in the air, showing Adam and Eve where to go as they left the garden. Together they prayed, "בָּרוּךְ אַתָּה יי אֱלֹהֵינוּ מֶלֶךְ הָעוֹלָם בּוֹרֵא מְאוֹרֵי הָאֵשׁ," thanking God for the creation of fire. Then, as they watched the shadows flicker, they realized that God made a world with הַבְדָּלָה in it. They knew that fire could not be created on Shabbat, but now it could. They thanked God for all the distinctions, ending בָּרוּךְ אַתָּה יי הַמַּבְדִּיל בֵּין קֹדֶשׁ לְחוֹל. This was the first הַבְדָּלָה. The next day Adam and Eve began to use the fire to cook, to keep warm, and as a tool.

(From *P.R.E.* 20 and various sources cited in Ginzburg, *Legends of the Jews*)

Questions

1. Why are people scared of the dark?
2. What is it like to look into a flame or a fire?
3. What did Adam and Eve learn from the first fire?
4. How can knowing this story help you to point your heart when you participate in הַבְדָּלָה?

1. הַמַּבְדִּיל בֵּין קֹדֶשׁ לְחוֹל, בֵּין אוֹר לְחֹשֶׁךְ

2. בֵּין יוֹם הַשְּׁבִיעִי לְשֵׁשֶׁת יְמֵי הַמַּעֲשֶׂה

3. הִנֵּה אֵל יְשׁוּעָתִי אֶבְטַח וְלֹא אֶפְחָד

4. לַיְּהוּדִים הָיְתָה אוֹרָה וְשִׂמְחָה וְשָׂשׂוֹן וִיקָר

5. בָּרוּךְ אַתָּה יי אֱלֹהֵינוּ מֶלֶךְ הָעוֹלָם בּוֹרֵא מְאוֹרֵי הָאֵשׁ

6. כֵּן תִּהְיֶה לָנוּ כּוֹס יְשׁוּעוֹת אֶשָּׂא וּבְשֵׁם יי אֶקְרָא

Can you see the three letters בדל in these words?

מַבְדִּיל   הַבְדָּלָה   לְהַבְדִּיל

מַבְדִּיל = separate

הַבְדָּלָה = service that separates
Shabbat from the rest of the week

לְהַבְדִּיל = to divide

קָדוֹשׁ

מַבְדִיל

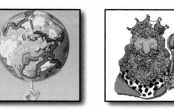

עוֹלָם

מֶלֶךְ

אַתָּה

בָּרוּךְ

אוֹר

חֹשֶׁךְ

יִשְׂרָאֵל

יוֹם

Your teacher will help you with your translation.

בָּרוּךְ אַתָּה יי אֱלֹהֵינוּ מֶלֶךְ הָעוֹלָם

הַמַּבְדִיל בֵּין קֹדֶשׁ לְחוֹל, בֵּין אוֹר לְחֹשֶׁךְ

בֵּין יִשְׂרָאֵל לָעַמִּים

בֵּין יוֹם הַשְּׁבִיעִי לְשֵׁשֶׁת יְמֵי הַמַּעֲשֶׂה.

בָּרוּךְ אַתָּה יי הַמַּבְדִיל בֵּין קֹדֶשׁ לְחוֹל.

My best guess at the meaning of this prayer is:

_____

_____

_____

_____

_____

_____

שְׁבִיעִי

שֵׁשׁ

עֹשֶׂה

Words

ordinary = חוֹל

nation = עַם

between = בֵּין

Word Parts

and = הַ

134

An Elijah Story

This story starts with a poor Jewish man who cries out to God. The man, though poor, is always good to other people. Elijah, dressed as an Arab merchant, comes to him and gives him two coins. The two coins build themselves into a fortune. The man becomes rich and forgets about others. He gets lost in his new wealth. The Arab merchant appears before the man again and demands the return of his two coins. When Elijah is paid back the man's fortune collapses. Again he is poor, but he returns to his kindness. The man again cries out to God, and this time Elijah appears before him dressed as Elijah and says, "I will make you rich again if you promise not to change the way you treat other people."

(drawn from Ginzburg, *Legends of the Jews*)

Questions

1. What is the lesson of this story?
2. What does it teach us about Elijah? How does it help us understand the connection between הַבְדָלָה and Elijah?
3. How does knowing this story help you to point your heart when you participate in הַבְדָלָה?

Another Elijah Story

Rabbi Yehoshua ben Levi met Elijah standing by the entrance of Rabbi Simeon ben Yoḥai's tomb. The rabbi asked Elijah, "When will the Messiah come?" Elijah answered, "Go and ask him yourself." Elijah took him to meet the Messiah, who was sitting with the lepers in the gates of Rome. All of the other lepers untied their bandages all at once and then rebandaged them all at once. The Messiah was undoing his bandages one at a time and changing one bandage before he undid the next. He was always ready to come if he was called. Rabbi Yehoshua asked, "When will you come?" He answered, "Today." The next day when the Messiah had not come, Rabbi Yehoshua returned to Elijah and said, "He lied to me." Elijah said, "He meant, 'I will come today if you will listen to God's voice.'"

(*Sanhedrin* 97b)

Questions

1. What is the lesson of this story?
2. Why is Elijah connected to הַבְדָלָה?
3. How can knowing this story help you to point your heart during הַבְדָלָה?